REMEMBERING ANIMALS

REMEMBERING ANIMALS

Brenda Iijima

NIGHTBOAT BOOKS
NEW YORK

EPIDERMAL LAYERS
WE ARE HERE

Printed in the United States
ISBN: 978-1-937658-49-6

Design and typesetting by HR Hegnauer
Cover collage by Brenda Iijima: *Reunion in Animal*, 2016

Cataloging-in-publication data is available
from the Library of Congress

Distributed by University Press of New England
One Court Street
Lebanon, NH 03766
www.upne.com

Nightboat Books
New York
www.nightboat.org

poems from *remembering animals* have appeared in: *colorado review*, *the volta*, *mandorla*, *how 2*, *octopus magazine*, *cannot exist*, *the tiny*, *wheelhouse magazine*, *face time anthology*, *tarpaulin sky online*, *war and peace anthology*, *cannibal magazine*, *2nd avenue poetry*, *fascicle*, *tzak journal*, *outside voices-four square*, and *poets for living waters*.

rabbit lesson was published as a chapbook by fewer and further press.

this book is dedicated to all animals.

TABLE OF CONTENTS

OPENING PHASE

birds where there were
birds where there were
birds where there were
birds were there once
birds *where there were*

the apparatus was never bird-like
was never never not bird-like
was not not bird-like
was not as bird-like
lyrical reminder/remainder caught up in sky

(add a) next era our animal
conceptualization of time

form faces

interface

questioning
interchange

being

form faces

bleeding nukes as chickens pile up—null one hole as an epidemic

...eed, ...ead

rodeo chokehold abettors—each fly an individual portrait

grief (*but see body see*)

satellites pick up the buzz in the jungle—all that is jungle burns

as it appeared from the lagoon, brackish

swarms around willows—timber longitudinal with mountains for

took in neck then broke

heretofore and forearm or for kinship ties—finding of buffalo

lay down burden

writhing alongside the putrefied pustule of skin pestilence

his limb monologue lamb's leg

conflict as defined by skin's response to microbes

around eyes, eggs

how abstraction displaces the visceral

resistance, sustenance binding

hemitropic, then not really

sheep blood, agar, gel hydrolysis

drone——heads to vanishing point, illusion

daughter parasite in the merozoite stage

déjà vu syntactic storms of an extortionist drone

council of worms

bleed semiotics one solid gold nugget

colonial commodity boomtown fences

the law perpetuates its ardor

catachresis

pointillist effect for a squid's skin late night electricity

lanl test shots were named after

here: rhythm inscription, the figure, flesh now

flying insects, fruits and vegetables

touch meets traction

tundra

homo tantum thrum

taiga

a blended nature, then thermonuclear, zaire pende mask

desert or dune

where there were portraits is the cacophony matrix

intraordinal

vectors like sampling

dimorphism, sexual

the animal-ready

other: urban, suburban, agricultural

ready animal scourge

riparian, estuarine, intertidal

birdshot blind lot forested consequence

terrestrial biomes

convened on a rock

arboreal scansorial terricolous

caricature oozes out perplexed identity

cursorial fossorial

jugular where politic intertwines river

files glides social colonial

anthropod vector of many myriads only few survived

spindletop

hoe and the head load

mammary glands, ribs, my nervous system

fractionalized anthropocene days

collocation

daughter nuclei, daughter parasite, the merozoite stage

pulverize the hush of dawn, reflected

red herring/drones/feed baby with royal jelly

one's mirror absolute

insects battle battle bilharzias

clambering fore/expunge/vanishing

wax, shellac, cochineal, silk, food, drink

iteration of official thought as the body acts

zoonosis: smote votive emerods golden "i removed

purring feathers little stresses

the carcasses" wrote ashurbanipal in annals

truckle all birds court the cat cringing

cat visage on kitchen towel

RABBIT LESSON

rabbits live peaceably in the briar——tallish underbrush for furry
bodies——forage thistle forage borage——escape invasion
struggle——foxes study plump meat——the rabbit is an animal
fox, animal   in the jungle——disembowel the
rabbit——demonstrates the commando
lieutenant sir,

fling organs onto classmates——the last lesson
extra-textual
guerrilla warfare
preparatory
the cuddly rabbit
was our companion
for three days
we grew attached
we grew attacked
the lesson is conveyed
when the instructor
requires slaughter
hurl its viscera
the baby rabbit's
as if it was trash
around the room
become cool
killing machines
become disconnected
and attacked
we kill as a
combinatory ideal

rabbit hole where rabbits sleep——where rabbits mate——where
rabbits nibble clover——where foxes sleep——where foxes run—
—where a fox kills a rabbit——for food——uneasiness as the
trees sway

scansion catch cannot swatch

shock observation:

don't talk without permission
tree limb forced into human orifice jaggedly sharp——tree limb—
—gnarled——line up on line——hiding behind——in under——
line up on line——fire from the hip—
hunter-killer team——surround and sweep——received fire——
take no casualties——wrangler jeep baby carriage, innocence is
asleep——deep sleep

diurnal torpor——is when——creatures——'deep sleep' for only
part of a———day——part of day depends on——what animal it
is———designated for———
state engagement———conflict

pick-up zones——drop off zones——in an area called wagon
wheel——
fair game——efficiency in an area called wagon wheel——how
you——
next door neighbor——destroy a village——you know your
orders——
there's no one there——to give the signal——turning into an
animal

innocence is hairy or furry, cuddly and possessive

silence (ing, ing, ing)   grief (garish, gardenish)
ambience (remorse)

pro——gression ——predator to patriot——sign dotted bullet——
level playing field——level——raze——burn cows——burn
houses——burn breathing bodies——
kill——a——rich——experience——seems a caper when sleep
deprived

unleash terror to put a nation to sleep
one man's safety is another man's living hell
struggle through thick foliage
stick a flag into the beating organ
there's no telling what
our boys are doing

all that has transpired
is minutely recorded
in living tissue
in cells of being
living history

blood-brain barrier——barracks

led to believe——training——weren——'t——hu——man——
lead——

we became animals——

————(when) did you cease to be an animal——?

lead with a gun butt——ad——minister

——con——s——id——er
in——trep——id
t——o——f——lay
——s——kin

——nimbleblowup——im——im——im——im——

brains hide hide slaughter——hide——animals——shells
cold mortar——armada fur, armada honoree, arm, arm
withstand atrocity
atrocious history standing

murmuring——whining
adverse,——animals
extraordinarily cut
the scent
envelops linen shrouds fetid traipsed

blood sweats into crevices like ice nice lakes like
faces

missed moiled demise dismissed enterprises apply

somewhere between 15 and 50
two digit numbers

we had a couple of guys—from philadelphia
in our squadron
they used to blindfold the guys
with safety wire
pull it real tight
with copper wire
tearing into their eyes and nose
and binding their hands
with safety wire
used to have contests
to see how far they could
throw the body
out of the plane
throw one as far as you can
and see if you can get the other one further

split

hairs

• • •

orders come from above

impulses come from internal mechanisms

contradiction/constriction

-bodily, boding

sovereign map of the brain

all been wiped out long ago

the young, beautiful boys slay

beautiful beautiful boys

they slay she says
frayed as he does
dazed these as

to western breasts clings camouflage

my limb like that empathy

limb slung in like that empathy

greenery underbrush
and leaves

owner's manual states shot to kill is a killing field is a duty for sovereignty is sanctioned endorsed essentiality of democracy to further such ideals to quell dissonant uprisings communal conditions bonding meld into rules other the animal and animalistic mobility as they run away into the underbrush pursuit to kill as many as they run toward or—trusting/thrusting

top brass

winter soldiers return home to cold shoulders
17,000 veterans are homeless
and subsist in the woods in Florida alone
kill manual pillow pillow fraught sleep pillow close company
confession is our national anthem
down to the last drop
rest easy
kill the pain
kill the approbation
kill the connotation
kill the fantasy
we sleep together as institutional sociality
being nice is an ongoing act
infuriate kindness
gentle gestures where designated

away wet dripping leaves underbrush guerilla maneuvers
i seek they sought to substantiate the body this act of reminding
about the body to remind the body of itself the body as a reminder
of specificities of action
accountable by bodies
stones evolve slowly stone
hurl fossorial local biota
predation causes significant mortality among mammals
are not exactly automatons could not be——per the events at
hand——per hands——per operative maneuver——per actions—
—per a concern like care
came down the hill
and blew all of the kids away
just blew all of the kids away
and just like *click response
they got up and just like *click
response
they just blew all the kids away
and the truck just continued down the hill
5 or 6 kids they just blew away
the lieutenant fired too, as the truck slowed down

war assimilates logical uncertainty
over spilling mortal coil
do not hold out hope for a looping into each other
our societal bodies literally shattered
asunder buckled injected
we make each other
we take each other
to pieces
a thesis

epidermal layers

vibrissae——under——brush——jitter
brackish——effected——viscera
richly innervated——littoral——carousel
————scared——not disparate
urge————urgent——vertical death
—————————— :

perceptions

neck break break neck referring to speed referring to bodily gesture hawk breaks lizard's neck——lightning

each

pour machine gun fire into a treeline to cover
napalm air strikes raise clouds
into gray monsoon skies as houseboats
glide down the perfume river
helicopter exhaust in faded light
humidity
strain on
vital
organs

each

feelings

breath

movement

landscape is terrain——to get through——edit——

——

muddy—— suck ankles in impressions of a running
body

epidermal fungal corrosive outer wall corruptible surface
shell

shelter
ditches
thick foliage
tangle

cawing birds mimic hammering——cause dimension——depth
perception

dense thickets of an anaconda dawn pink——stretches
enfolds——stretches

the scratchy underbrush vivid green continuum khaki sidles against
this green
bodily green

——wade ashore with heavy equipment——

hawk's foresight——big rock to drop cadaver——down on——

——

——

terminus peculiarly————rocks————hunger————sky,
falling

a mouse in falcon's beak, pressed there bulging viscera pressing
against sharp clamped beak flown above valley a falcon swooped
from high altitude
from lower branch of a tree——somewhere sky stealthy hungrily
gingerly a mouse was foraging daily when——

——when **salt lick**
whale bone
quick, gone

when————

dissonance——distance——body: yourself, body, fur: yourself, —
—distance
is not approximation, is your fur, your body hair, your skin——
your,——self
as it appears reflected up from the lagoon,
brackish, the lagoon, thick with the weedy, sticky, rotting mixture,
like oil, dense and tangled, lagoon, where eyes stare, eyes see eyes
these tangles, the lagoon, so tired——body——
lagoon sees bones they are reflected upwards down from river
where the body was
left the body there
by that huge trunk of a tree
where the lagoon
was
body eyes **silence (ing, ing, ing)**
grief (garish, gardenish)
ambience, remorse

around the body animals roam it is unclear what
what they are doing (not with the body) they are autonomous
but see body see

i personally used clubs, rifle butts, pistols, knives
and this was always done at
hill 29
the important thing is
everything i did was
always monitored

maybe they take a bite from it **like ice nice lakes like faces**
bite their teeth into it
into that body flung there
after all it is blood and skin and fur
it is meat
do they take a bite from it
or maybe there isn't hunger just now
depart from it
subsistence on a body
not this sort of meat
torpor whisper
torpor or whisper dazed
bones between life rising
torpor or whisper
dazed
bones thank you, bones
living oh, living oh
body not quite dead slack against
trunk
heaving shocked fatal
injury incurred
before the lagoon trauma
the body pays for strife
with trauma
and here is that body as an image against a tree dense death or

dying blood flowing a state of mind i could not know my limb like
that slung i can see this in an image and its of trauma and the trauma
is to sack action the person is absorbed into the body

                                   the tree collects moisture in this case rain
                        sweat blood urine stinging eyes open she——
                        random not random from the closest village——of
                        an age to——
opening eyes——from

                                                       girl, so woman
fur yanked off

nothing happens can nothing not happen language not nothing
nothing not happening

greenery, underbrush, leaves

what art envisions

overlap in image

i assume she was raped
that's pretty SOP
standard operating procedure

you have to realize fully
what you've been taught

pure light event in color

human being human described as follows with nothing else on stage

"help me! help me!"

hyperbole of indexical information administration of distress
sunken, shifted **instinct thinks**

girl cloud presence to die preclude
what

death so this happens a sampling this is war or killing or action in the underbrush

law whipped lair

compression vessel
augury steam
the inner lung

a killing action
summarizes language
missed moiled demise dismissed
violence nominal **sadness, grieving envelops**
violence seminal

cranium liberté
fallen in inflamed large
stoked was his brother **my limb like that**

slung into underbrush
slung in—empathy

grieving envelops

strife auditorium
sad can't summarize sanity
war works machinery

flag-draped coffins stationary by runway

dog finds her
body dog
finds
her
is a dog
lives in this village
isn't wild
a dog
licks her
the body

licks her, the body
burn burning smell
leaves ignite
welter
smoke soaked by slightest wind mood
chemical residue
sparkling toxins coat skin forest fields
"ranch hand" c-123 aircraft spray
liquid defoliant
the four specially
equipped planes
covered a 1,000-foot-wide
swath in each pass

over the dense vegetation
coat houses
an agent so strong it melts limbs
soil and sediment
biomagnification

wind promotes gasoline to flare **rocks, hunger**
the sky falling

fiber lights up

it is hers clothes

doesn't burn so easily tree, nor dirt nor
child
requires ignition

eyes

like an
animal spit roasted
shank

charcoal clump **musculature atrophied, caved in,**
they look vulnerable without their clothes on
gelled incendiary device to melt mortal coil
where does the dog go now
where
does the dog go
now
only animals
slither in the murk of the lagoon thick
serpentine spidery fish-like deepening
only animals
hunt around the periphery of the lagoon thick
oily eye the lagoon sees sun sees sky rifle sees explosion
there's a large river that runs north and south of saigon
i can't remember the name of it

vestigial hind legs
pelvic girdle slither elliptical pupils
sex, skeptical hind legs

pit viper asian cobra coral
krait snake with satchel charge **juicy larvae reveal their flavors**
single row of plates

swaying
tangle

lungs are of plants
the pool is of speech

sing stung oviduct
whiplash rifle butt

mop up meat
mop up that meat!
perceptual inputs
mop meat up
motor outputs

mop mop mop up meat!

cavalry division infantry division bush land mosaic captivated
battalion

hammer my mammary glands
anvil
my motor hammer my mammary glands
pleasure my anvil

later on another action other space or setting other underbrush or
same
viper kills dog

modified by half-moon light

pleasure me
warm blooded _______________
pleasure me
warm blooded creature
(they grow in dim light)
pinging densities
bodily, boding

hometown gun metal
meat in the back and fuel lobes we
cut for collective
futures—— ——tracking device by skull bones

out here the tension just builds
and builds
until you feel
like you are going to explode

torpor or whisper dazed bones
thank you
——in view, brambles

the men must cut their way through
8 foot tall razor sharp elephant grass
and bamboo covered in thick thorny vines
the countryside is also infested with thousands
of poisonous insects and snakes
ambushes and booby traps
search it fast
this is a job
they quickly realize
destroy it fast

earlobes **to hear out interiors** dynamism rings hold on
cataclysm
interior is gone——imploded hardened softened corroded sickened
impinging
self-scintillating
senses disconnect except for metal——slobber——under shower—
—regimented spasm
breath frothing basis————————————————time was
sincere
really hyperreal ————torpor or whisper————
—

they were promised water, water

mud slung naturalistic ————an historic——
——

humming gunning ————toucan
chirping————

a living room in combat gear in living
room a combat gear

how met you hot (animal) feel

homeopathy

subtle hollow ignoble blob with future effect
(our invention!)

culled from another's anatomy
or smeltingly molten fusion uranium ticking nuclear device an
corrosive!

organ of elimination
stricken with classification
a substance to blush with blush
out of skin
your rose flesh

portrait's impulses

birch, chocolate, deeper shades
your rose flesh ample
under epidermal layer
light and pressure loosely cursive

suggestive lacunae

materials: tar, feathers

remixing surface dimensions
and raw and gnaw

lack or excess/of meaning/of meat

pelting season   hold—on—to—the—form

______chained to ______ rather cavalierly

tatty and botched

in the center of a perfectly sterile room the oozing oxen

girded, intractable neck

———the

satellites to y/our laden blood link up with y/our contours
neighborhoods embedded, gates mere specks
at the cellular level the atrocities are metropolises
merging poison with water water
merging fire with poison poison

remixed surface dimension and raw or gnaw

even the air

stinks of human

waste

war can't be separated from *where* where can't be separated from
what what can't be separated from *all* can't be separated from y/our
jugular vein your spinal cord y/our *animal dignity*y/our *pow-*
er excess can't be separated from *excess* from excess from excess
from *loss* the *loss of the environment* can't be separated from
the production of calm and the production of sweat and the
production of desire

spurn on

he thinks he's been out here so long
he knows everything there is to know

beauty from *rhetorical gestures* from *theoretical speech* from
intimacy from *splendor y/our autonomy can't be separated from*
y/our autonomy what y/our reality/y/our reality from y/our passion
ion tons or words

kill zone hill 937

cellular kinship strip strip insulation its distance immunity strip

desert melted meat guns they fired off from shoulder length the sun
blazed on the digital maps in strokes of circuitry the enemy falters
in terminology can't be said to resemble water can be said to
resemble water substitution for water substitution for oxygen
substitution for li
fe
o
r

<table>
<tr><td>w</td><td>e</td><td colspan="7">citatory conundrums</td></tr>
<tr><td>r</td><td>e</td><td>a</td><td>s</td><td>o</td><td>n</td><td>f</td><td>o</td><td>r</td></tr>
<tr><td></td><td>l</td><td>i</td><td>f</td><td>e</td><td colspan="4">i fraying</td></tr>
<tr><td></td><td>s</td><td></td><td></td><td></td><td></td><td></td><td></td><td></td></tr>
<tr><td>i</td><td>t</td><td>z</td><td>n</td><td>p</td><td>f</td><td>g</td><td>s</td><td>m</td></tr>
<tr><td></td><td colspan="8">y horizon</td></tr>
<tr><td></td><td>a</td><td>q</td><td>l</td><td>b</td><td>x</td><td>i</td><td>z</td><td></td></tr>
</table>

by usual, the hair standing on itself

nouns accents air

iota noticeable
significance spatially separated, can it
can't
gaps of inner surface   poverty so there's only only
and then only
poverty duress so homelessness
pressure release shrapnel blast
nearly 1 million injured GI are airlifted in medevac helicopters
numbers abound: the damage done

jugular intertwines frontlines

dogged whatnot dusted corneas

trawling unmatchable resplendent with razor wire

heavy metal aural and pepper   saline   cleaning out

the soldiers thought of the soldiers thought of

over and out big house

road to basra road to treblinka road to the pentagon, road to a
reservation, an internment camp in nevada—expulsion: al-nakba,—
speak historically, right around here holding tank nerve flank to
freeze strategic truths out of loins

eyes cry for you

a trail of tears

CERTAIN
CURTAINS
SHIFT

collectively by the anterior
explanation surge——abyss told in verse
a realism that looks steely——really——really
stumble out of animal stumble into capital
grapple with power grapple with perception
heart pounding bastion of concentration
the realm of mannerisms made modern mammals
along came an imperceptible interval
hungering, that's what we do
endless production line
tableau emphasizing emanation

dealing directly with charismatic animals

as they bestride color

—coloration

no longer the cannibal teen

nerve lions say sign language
vet, bleat, sling
so we slink down
coyly as soap
glides glandular
marshalling afternoon mist
(so that) (effect)
certain curtains shift
tune étude to ear of seahorse
lobe under kneecap scenting
oozing
we hot twigs
steam
hush winter s tumbles v apor

we are
here
we are
here we
are here
we are
here we

birthm
ark
stuck by essential hist
ory
—itten that is wildernesses backward look
ing
redactor
puzzles with exaggerated narration

the nouns the nouns: mask, space, skin

COROLLARY

forefathered, directly from bodies

grandfathered into clauses

in today's parlance, a wishing well

aggression profusion | grievances | disparagement | presences

vortex of war

violence built into skin

anomalous energy

aggravations of tone

PHANTOM LIMB ORCHID

it hurt like a mitt or muff

thou art bunny
a finer friend one cannot conceive

ms. bunny and mr. peebles (hedgehog)
please step this way and accept the honor of this prize

i raced down the hill to my burrow. there i found an empty
warren—chester and willis were off chasing mice…

the boy told me how cute
i looked and i blushed

whisker to whisker
before language we could only whimper…

a raw maneuver to cut off the wrists
idle, though the tail is
slouch scourge was, the three dangling iron spikes
mental shock caused by black death
so that you become swollen and blue
fallen of teeth
song birds don't want god to see them
eat   bunting
drowning alive in armagnac
bones symbolize soul
eat under a sack
lol aromas captures

here: rhythm inscription
the figure is flesh now
touch meets traction

[suchness] [soft meats]

scapegoated by the wells   women [witches]
          grandmothers [ours]   jews [you and i]

the water source was universal meaning one well in a communal
space   fear contaminates   townships prepare the
burning pyres   fumes flames spitting fire

branded as a social group [hematological characteristic]

how are our elbows different [really]   [outfoxed]

the fish gene in me presently balks

according to stephen m. meyer, author of *the end of the wild:*
"and while 10,000 tigers live as pets in the united states, fewer than
7,000 live in the wild throughout the world!"

each gyration scared the flock

all appellations in these domains———are omitted

culturally derisive, derided——————————
discussion of health————discriminatory campaign to categorize
people by their health issues————————————policy
insinuates health is an elite status [reserved for the rich]

[was normative] [what is] [was] [norm] [how normative are norms
ever really] [endocrine disturbances universal] [asthma for everyone]
[up the food chain] [not *you* !]

a fine animal, i assure you
formidable fine and fair
foiled fomented tribunal
fraught
forlorn
fraught internal mechanism
fraught foil
fulsome
freaked out

CORPORAL

sac of blood that body is

that *that* body

here's when the
                    the body

maximizes bodies——count

——blur

etymology shel——ter——"charlie, it's a pretty good-sized ape"

broiler————differentiate your DNA structure————there's
an animal loose in the basement————regressed to some quasi-
simian creature————out of a group of five primate subsets——
——i was utterly primal

check the boiler room————neurologically intact————i
couldn't go in because of the lizards————who's the attending
radiologist? ————world panic————baboon vocalization—
———architecture somewhat abnormal————baboons are
carnivorous

  gymnasium trees swing with ease
locked into function where the thumbs wore out

      decided slip of punctuation, grammar, syntax
diction   club-like   fake skinned head
     self-determination cuts butter   *better*, upright
 or trot   my limb like that   wince, whence
        growl   red circles   concentration: predatory position
                    moon shines on fangs
                            owl not a lot
                   skeptical hind
                        legs
                    the sex
                  truncated
                      ears receded
         the ape and the mirror faded

go out on the town TONGUE
and stuck his elbow out
townships stuck to this edict
it was said they went OUT OF THEIR WAY
the descriptive word came in handy
for jungle bungle effect cracked sidewalk
WITHout hesiTATION my instinct thinks
look how they appear without CLOTHES

THEY LOOKED VULNERABLE WITHOUT CLOTHES ON
musculature atrophied caved in biceps sunken shifted

WITHOUT CLOTHES ON THE ANIMAL RESEMBLANCE
ancestral table of CONTENTS

the ape helped the man get a cup of coffee
he, quadriplegic

bobcat
come lately
carcass
feeding
tiger pen
one of the last
remaining snow
leopards
zoo?

BEHIND BARS CONSCIENCE

aprendere a luchar desde esta celda, esta sera mi trichera.
[i will learn to struggle from this cell. this will be my trench.]
nidia díaz, *nunca estuve sola*

conscience ~~is the call of care wrote heidegger~~
for the uncanny he said was said
was said to say and published
of being-in-the-
world that summons to be
to its own most potentiality-for-being-guilty
behind bars latent in cage
zoological trope strips criminality of brutality excess access hoax (caging) these men
society sees anachronistically
he notates where legislated
wanting-to-have-a-conscience corresponded to understanding summons
and he elaborates that both these characterizations are not immediately harmonious
with the vulgar interpretations of conscience
i state that time out of time
i state this lockup sucking
this state sanctioned apparatus
white lockdown condition conditioning eugenic industrial model
torture emblem cruelty
this state created implementation
this razor wire racism
social creation
social control
socialization
animal
when i
the stuffed
animal

animal morale

the underground is blown

pain/constrain

they weren't sleeping… "her autobiography opens as she lies semiconscious, chained to a bed in a heavily guarded hospital room, recalling the incident: 'there were lights and sirens. zayd was dead. my mind knew that zayd was dead. the air was like cold glass. huge bubbles rose and burst. each one felt like an explosion in my chest. my mouth tasted like…'"
assata shakur's *assata: an autobiography*

dogs were sent in to inhibit the uprising. trained to intimidate they aggressively charge forth once unleashed (how did we bleed) the dogs are used in prisons in riot scenarios usually racial the dogs are used to sniff out suspects, criminals, drugs, at the border dogs maintain the gates, (that meat, presently held down by a fork and knife) a dog is a perfect component of the family unit, a loving companion there at one's beck and call (where does the elegy lead) keep it in a cage all day while you are at work, the dog persists, in a dangerous situation, dog

<u>estivation</u> is
another form of <u>torpor</u>,
dormancy, or "sleep"

animals that estivate are trying to escape things happening in their environment. this happens in hot desert climates where heat and water are so important to the animals that live there. estivation protects these animals from high temperatures and drought.

just as animals hibernate in order to stay alive in cold places, animals estivate [or aestivate] in hot, dry places. the bodies of estivators will slow down. breathing and heartbeat get very slow. the animal doesn't need as much food and water to live since food is fuel for energy and they aren't using much. reptiles use 90-95% less energy when they are estivating. animals don't move, grow or eat during this time.

'…blood and dirt. the car spun around me and then something like sleep over took me. in the background i could hear what sounded like gunfire. but i was fading and dreaming…'
assata shakur's *assata: an autobiography* continued…

regarding the cormorant:
crow hawk eagle vulture
susan howe quotes milton's *paradise lost*, when she states,
cardinal redwinged blackbird raven chicken
"milton makes the bird a similitude for satan."
rooster turkey turtledove pigeon hummingbird

peacock nightingale mockingbird goose   harlequin quail   eat crow

"so clomb this first grand
thief into god's fold;/ so
since into his church lewd
hirelings climb./ thence
up he flew, and so on the
tree of life, / the middle
tree and highest there
that grew, / sat like a
cormorant, yet not true
life/thereby regain'd, but
fat deviling death/to them
who liv'd; nor on the
virtue thought/of that
life-giving plant, but
only us'd/for prospect,
what well us'd had been
the pledge/of immortality.
So little knows/any, but
god alone, to value right"
john milton, *paradise lost*

spread eagle

don't tread [snake]

on me

when hot and dry times come, estivators will find themselves a safe place to sleep——usually underground. this is the only way some animals can live through high heat and no water.

some examples of estivators are:

when i was 19, 18, 17——turning into an animal——
there was a reason

treason, of animal the human

being over beings imbibed beings with fur without fur

gadfly flout

compensate

the dictum

revoke

an animal turns in ward

sick

pitted lives in

cave against

other

(each)

bravery is

THE THREE RAVENS

HEART
GLOWING
PUPILS

this is the softer, more sentimental tale with a merry refrain:
down a downe

one of the three

ravens tells a

tale of true love   a knight is

dead in the meadow, and a doe,
                heavy with child, sees him

she kisses his wounds and buries
him,
then dies
herself—

she kisses him all over
ravenously
studies his organs
his cock is symbolic—
thus beauty is originated
apples begin to grow on
trees
as her powers became
internalized—
this is, allegorically
the image
of tragedy
and a thesis concerning
power
conceptually buttressing ideas of
of "true love"
in western canonized form
oh, sie, xie

is moi
hir is sire
all are quite sure
the ravens indicate
a feudal daydream
she can overwrite it
and rework it
a tragedy is refusal
she refuses this fatal narrative
yet she dies nonetheless
the precedent poses immense pressure

fucking is grand
interplay
but
what did they mean
by symbolically rendering
gender and class dynamics
by submerging bodies
into deer and doe

tuxedoed men armed with guns
arrive

undercover contracted killers arrive

they represent multinational corporations
the dow is down

they are extralegally there

a more ominous reading

they depart in unmarked vehicles
discreet presences
almost impossible to notice
within the day's trajectory
signifying

the embarrassment of
for-profit manipulations and
historical fortifications
careening forth into a future
that orients itself in failure

the arousal of money
its awakening properties
kleig lights
amplify the confusion

at the bus stop
down is down

thrashing/fist fight/slash

she out cold in the mud items from her purse strewn about
about this there is no mention hair torn by temple
there are deer in the woods outnumbered
murder takes place in the field
the body lies hidden in a stagnant ditch
local authorities come too late
cheap romp sideways dastardly masterful what seems romantic
exactitude perfect lips clit nipples there dappled sunlight leaves
brush fronds lingering light racing tripped up stone rocks and rot the
spinning trickle brook to valley running racing flow they found
what was botched innocence an idea easy light she young with bow
in the hills behind the wasted encampment smoking arrows there run
three boys gouge out her eyes

that's what ms. lucy said

ravens in the trees overhead

in one's own childhood, abridged
brooks flowed were mountain streams
bodies glistened in mercury baths
chatter illogically logical to inner tones of rocks, faults

i did and with my sister traverse roofs and
in back garden to forest gradient an expanse no longer evident
titillate the rocks
blood and dirt were inseparable

during that time
the town held the nation's per capita statistic
for murder
each woman
whether strewn as remains somewhere in the remote of mountain
dumpster, clothes closet, hotel trash dispenser
container, contents, contained
—teenage pregnancy highest in this town nationwide same year
to endure, generally a struggle for deer
the hounds and the hawk suffice

THREE RAVENS (grimoires)

night creature, screech owl
or how lilith was subsumed into a pentagram
and took the visage of a goat
and what this has to do with the leviathan
and who is samael
will he speak gently
will he speak

opposition of good and evil is indicated through the
inverted triangles like flags the opposition flutters
tongues clap signals
binaries don't show the gracious hosts they are to the
dissident whose symbiosis swings tails
the underbrush is an overgrown grove
as when ouroboros bites its own tail
trapezoid red motivates nature
sleep flung space warbles
the knife drops into the lamb of sight
can be seen in a chunk of meat
    heart with its glowing pupils
    pupa spun into change
    dark energy for faces
    pulses for carcasses
    unraveled aortas
    satellite end her sleep is light
    low decibels, dense travel
    the thickness of hydrogen plasma
the lamb is our substitution/sacrifice/body to appease
[she was] divided into parts from, ostensibly adam's rib, missing
missing referent

    the lungs are of plants
    in the pool is speech

HUMANIMAL, FURRY

cranium tuft at the conference we were bonded
indigo   bloodletting you little rabbit so polyester
soft
to want to be an animal
to want to be stuffed
cute and puffy
sometimes they had the wings of a bat or bird, or the body of a dog

what am i am
when i
am i
am

meow
informational

meow club

i don't swim like a fish, i am a fish

cognitive kitten kitten coalition kitchen kitten paw claw kitten mr.
kitten lives on the second floor adjacent from another mr. kitten,
part pumpkin part beast

scintillating long necked whale shark glamour regal of squid go to
chain retailer to buy the fur used whale bone to make my fangs kill
a chicken with my teeth when i sleep it is in a nest

in my case it is to a stone that i aspire
i remain inert for hours, days

i like the animal to climb over

animals often ignore rocks

climb out of car kangaroo

fantastical limbo with long ears

working——————like a dog

watch dawg

dog days dog-id, chubby chubby piggy, sow

meandering ocelot, snout, cut, root out **sentimentality in the form of hazard green lizards**

under the oed entry 'orc':

1605 j. SYLVESTER tr. g. de s. du bartas *deuine weekes & wks.* (II. i. 337) "insatiate orque, that euen at one repast, almost all creatures in the world would waste." [seeming 'orca' usage]

lab rat/guinea pig/test monkey

cybernetic animal proxy fighter

drones to mimic swarms

pond frogs and lamas

genetically modified potato spliced with DNA from the snowdrop plant drop dead is poisonous to mammals
damage to the rat's stomach lining yummm
mayonnaiseyuuuummmketchupbovinegrowthhormoneudd
erwondergeneengineermonsantodupont
agrohormonaltoxicpesticides for snacks

butter-/

flies/boar/o/daisy cutters

in/

distance

CHEETAH HUNTING (click here to read about Leopard hunting)

If you are looking for a **Cheetah hunt** take into consideration that we have the highest density of Cheetah population in the world right where Ozondjahe Hunting Safaris game reserve is located. Our **Cheetah hunting** trophy pictures speak for themselves, click **here** to view our **Cheetah hunting pictures** or click **here** to view our **African hunting trophy** photo gallery.

"the closest i've come to getting a handle on all of this is something painter eric fischl has talked about. imagine calling two pets, one a dog the other a cat. asking a dog to do something is an amazing experience. you say, 'come here, fido,' and fido looks up, pads over, puts his head in your lap, and wags his tail. you've had a direct communication with another species; you and fido are sharing a common, fairly literal language. now imagine saying, 'come here snowflake' to the cat. snowflake might glance over, walk to a nearby table, rub it, lie down, and look at you. there's nothing direct about this. yet something gigantic and very much like art has happened. the cat has placed a third object between you and itself. in order to understand the cat you have to be able to grasp this nonlinear, indirect, holistic, circuitous communication. in short, art is a cat.

jerry saltz, village voice, september, 2006

jane goodall yell

language degenerated into rule(s)

complexity compressed into a finite mesh (ouch!) (my skin won't accept this restraint) the wolves at whipsnade, phaedrus my ass

said cells made me do it said cells dictate, science syndicated indicates tendency and behind each modulation an ideology

one droplet of beast

selfsame pterodactyl treacle eradicate (keyword)

"at this point champions of philosophic egoism tend to cry 'humbug!' and stop listening."

mary midgley, *beast and man*

what is a centaur then?

how will you have your ham?

TENDENCY

hammer anvil stirrup
———hair
mammary glands
mop up meat

the next war begins
for those who survived

homeopathy

perceptual inputs
motor outputs

fusillade
gardens of meat pumpkins——husband harvests them
(his invention)
so that the source of
protein
won't involve
the killing of
warm-blooded crea—
tures
you just
roll
them off
the shelves
(they grow in dim light)
and they are ready to har—
vest
devour
utopist interlude, a live recording
objects dim
damnable options abject

a contortion of the living room
splendor in soil
sugar cane burns as well as oil

bolder soulside
microstructural aura
dweller repeller
drunkenness sunkenness
corrosion   big rumbling noise in a stream   worn
rock
triptych depicts body curves
finalize with effervescence
the kid gets a sugar high
what *can* the brain say

frogs tell it
snakes tell
it
hawks tell it
the rhinos tell it
orangutans tell it
so too, and down the line
the telling with the body
so that where is the self located
***easy* on the remains**

reciprocity for the engine

what was considered the everyday

life

as we talked of freedom and justice one day for all, we sat down to steaks. i am eating misery, i thought, as i took the first bite. and spit it out.

alice walker, *"am I blue?"*

SHORN OF ITS HABITAT

as if a final descent HABITUATION RABBIT
the primeval swamp
the common herd
the crowded giant suns HOVERS THE NORM
the many questions posed
the many species written off
the most helpful people
in fact, the several individuals
in fact, their sense of loss ENTREAT
TREATY TREATMENT SUCKER
QUARREL THESE CLAWS
in fact, there's no way to measure
in fact, an international team
in fact, cremation, autopsy reports
in fact, *temporalities*
in fact, something to do with microeconomics SUCK UP
TO THE FACTS
in fact, the winning lottery ticket
in fact, regurgitation paragons
JUGULAR BONE BREAK HETEROTOPIC OSSIFICATION
bipedal apes
with opposable thumbs
without notice
the way tires squeal THE ANIMAL, SHE FELL OUT
OF A TREE
the way the day ends on the trading floor
the way you handle that device
the way advice is given WAS MOTHER
because where i live
where they live WAS MY MOTHER
where they live— SWARM AND FESTER
eternity of continuation
a flea, a parasite, a rat, a worm
a tick, a slug, a mouse FEEDING BY DAY
easter bunny numb
WHITE CHOCOLATE MOCHA ROYALE BITTER SWEET
DARK

TRICK

metronome more water—trick

suggestion trick, amplification trick

the rose of flesh oozes, yes it does *ohhhhhhs*

calculable figures swim loosely

light & pressure loosely cursive

hazard assemblages

—subconscious—subliminal—vicariously

automatic muscles of the animal

intervals too brief to be processed by the conscious mind

—because of the aversive responses

the untamable

didn't mention analogous

poems were peopled

wil(d)dēornes

•

surrounds carried off

a biological system hidden by mirrors, retina

to synthesize your response, an embryo

sequestered by invisible trees, the

adventure that took place without

consciousness, beauty, glistening beauty

roses, melting roses

panther, protect and savor

[growl]

self-administered to weaken

no, i mean strengthen

•

convert sound to sound
sound
and sounds around land land

face shivers face lassitude singing faces
the leaves collectively attached

pinging densities
sonar signals amid squalls

sound constellations move away
consilience—sensitivity jitters

spatial complexities of ideas
resemble thickets of briar, underbrush

a rampart few paces from the ordinary door
…screech owl whose ordinary retina

in the kitchen the data
entropy, communication

a knife handle
the teeming overhead lamp molecular

•

before the die
the bide, bidden

wetland vegetation/inner cortex/cortés/sea of cortez
squids of that sea
implanted like the private sector/sensor

petri dish
instinct of culture
…a most specific bacteria

admonish each member
nerve endings splayed
retreat to safest part on the bed, school

the sign on the door read
experience on the flipside
evidence

magnetism
pulls me toward your mind
          erotic language, tongue

•

please, with jazz inflection

as pressure has it, phased

image pressed on either side eater other

chiaroscuro by time

time backward time

wallop orb

op-ed

especially

culled miniscule relation w/subatomic meaning

behind spatial fires/wires twitch

getting back/to

our brethren

our breath and

brea
thing

•

thank you's that follow skyline linger
not linear backbone spinal cylindrical

lodge responses heartfelt inkling
light ooze lightness ossify bones between

bones between living and life/rising
bones, thank you living, oh and

sharing rids counting
counting without caring as caringly as can
saying w/out layer of chagrin
cajole odes oak modes to the core
oh yeah and

•

down by being been being as in a war or conflict like that
that
‘cuz to agitate the molecules you
when you split it down to that
imploding white light/fright
it kills the everything known as life

it is a transmitted idea
imploring a dominance
let loose a critical switch as when
back when time seemed still

still future
still past
still stillness
                    reverberation from the aftermath]

FLIGHT, FLIGHT

labyrinth of skin skin helps contain is in   inside time and in
outside time and out   a swallow enters in   shaft wall
solid shift   flail find rainbow tides   find found
railroad hides   dare i dare i   derelict idyll idyllic eyes
      now   underground feather falling where failing wailing
falling is fierce   burial nominal not to mention   shallow
within dirt   manumission
not to mention   oh there was a chair and chore and
consequence oh   that chair that choir that consequence that
terror that chord that consequence   there that there was a stair
      a child a glitter guttural   modulation crossing caring
got up sat down got up sat down down down down consequence
there was was was was was was was not to mention
so as to trail and tear and torn and this child that child consequence
now we and i and you and consequence
own that chain of consequence
condone that chain of consequence
clone that chain of consequence

oh i know consequence consequence
you know, protect that neck
you know, farm yard foreign
you know, a hatred glowing
and a river flowing
what *hot hot* about that encampment embankment
detention concentration invasion paralysis
what about that kitchen sitting talking saying
what about that school or those rules or that saying
a chomping bit how about children being beings being
how about a menace in the form of exploitation
we are!
she's!
they're!
he's!
getting on with a morning

oh, in the mind agate addenda affix
agitate innuendo but a scar says all
leather bound that says liptinite
waxy, waxy, resinous   and the mine is deep into mountain rock
tolerance   lingering like the residue of symptom
trade places with horse
intern in hunger hundreds plus plus hundreds
hundreds reconciliation looks like ink
language looks like an ax or feather
look away look at and towards
outer limit   l o o k   i n t o

she might have looked proper in her festive frock sipping tea
looking on saying nothing,
she might have conducted her inner rebellion on the swing
while watching bluebirds sing inside her
she was property of a patriarchal system
she did have voice
she was white like paste
she was gone like
she was going on

coal mine shaft meaning could be shifting
canary's

eyes staring   isn't disbelief   deeper skeptical attention
with traps like that   suspension   and tribulation
resistance formed with silence and a metal headdress
troll the savanna the boxcar the bus yard the courtyard
once dancing once dissolution and dancing dissolution and
talk that coagulates   vein   spine   cranium
breach   adversary   mainstream
street corner   high meadow   local foci
repertoire called bootlegging

concessions like ice cubes
lowdown what's up top
that's for sure

crosses crossing arms
planted along roadside stretches rural country fiery focus favoring
fear
bleed alongside the imperial
and then some
the apparition of harmony mutiny scrutiny
certitude with instructive attitude milieu henchmen largesse
leave skin deep quagmire out outed ousted otherwise impedes
change
the same man who sells shackles as souvenirs is dying of lung
cancer subverted thoughts, blindfolded, blindfolded
the whiteness is a dead zone undercover of broad daylight
making is rough
brush lips with contrition
tight fists might crawl to open imagine
interlock a-reckoning
dogma quaking

1847

there is perhaps not any condition in which human nature may be viewed in a more revolting aspect than that of a crowded slave vessel with dysentery on board.

portrayal, europa those fathers settle, mangle, mettle
mostly coastal, costly contrivances dazzle metal unutterable cargo
portrayal
happened one fine day jacquard ornamental full throttle hull mast ocular
white bird tamed wings sings songs not but fraught tight dawn creole
winds flap flag a sugar factory vision incursion
matchsticks resemble torsos when cargo cry out long triggering his
tory dent indented commission commiseration at the top of our
lungs
gushingly
gagged gushing the lungs
portrayal

---

of all the horrors attending the middle passage, with exception perhaps of smallpox, it is the worst. the effluvium which issues from her decks, or rather prisons, is peculiar and sickening, by any conception, and is generally perceptible at a great distance leeward.

a. bryson, *the sickness and mortality of the squadron on the african station*

leery o
f other *imported*! Differentiate your mother mother soothes you
downy delusional strict comfort
able wailing o majuscule jumbo
lingo linger
rage anguish
henchmen citizen law abiding states making trees do your dirty
work
compelling spit of history
thunder eagle bear
rain shower badger hare
fox ravine
forms of violence conceivable
meted out
stone as you push it water as you push it
because was because is
affect effect address panther black

---

of about 1 million men engaged in the american civil war, perhaps twice as many died of disease as were killed in battle. the federal armies lost 93,443 men killed in the battlefield or died of wounds, and 186,216 who died of disease. of the latter, 81,360 deaths were due to dysentery and typhoid fever. accurate figures for the confederate armies are not available, but it is known that disease accounted for an even higher proportion of casualty among men.

she was wearing an ear and a deformed fing
er a knee buckle of sk
ull had a striped shirt stripped a
way maybe flaming
spitted speak placard said never give testimony
against a
without a lantern
the cat o' nine tails
scrap of reproduction
man that ship shaped ship shapes
indigo bunting
sugar shaped like a brandish
she drowned in collect pond
her reflection did
not

---

of the diseases responsible for maintaining the isolation of africa for so long, malaria, dysentery, and yellow fever have been extremely important; but the influence of trypanosomiasis has probably been even more decisive. not only does it affect man in the form of sleeping sickness, but trypanosomiasis kills cattle and horses, which, consequently, can't be used

fetch the firkin
the fucking firkin buttering plunge
firkin butter that firkin wooden
metal cylindrical rim makes butter firm as in a firkin
i will not bust my hip churning
butter your buttons corporal punishment
while the milk is burning butter is smoldering
rancid lard implement and historicization neatly tucked
filed so the glass shows no finger prints
yes blood matches interior paint chip
yes blinded eyes match a schema of partitions
torture staid presented like tartan plaid civic criminal
minimal didactically accesses itself to squelch revolution
deborah squash's elegy
tarnishes wash
ing
tonnage
she revealed

---

for transport

they (others) (saw) (me) killing
without consciousness killing simply in stepping

(after) image (before) image

i stepped onto the tuft of grass (grassland)

spinal mantel crushing legs antennae several flew away
several others crawled away maimed others mangled in gel and
carcass forms muted

on the lawn ling
er
legs

molded by history
my legs move through thick grass
one step removed from my identity as a form of property
one step removed from fatality
one step removed from epiphany
one step removed from ancestry
one step removed from the license
to kill license to call to calm

---

in equatorial africa. the southward penetration of islam and its
culture would probably have extended much further had not the
horses of the faithful been killed by “nagana”, the deadly
trypanosome disease of domesticated animals.

j.l. cloudsley-thompson, *insects and history*

APPARITION—
WHAT'S STANDING RIGHT THERE

a repellent thing a very pretty
t h i n g
gertrude stein, three portraits of painters

d electable limb shook of plasma and veins
corpuscular bulge muscular from the chin to the ear
a neck lance
she merges with stereoscopic visionary fidelity
dearest of dear captivity narrative
they slept all day after day as escape transmission
lull
where the minute rendition of a jasper spear

quickens the hunt □$_{kl}$ = □e$_{rr}$ □$_{kl}$ + (2
mastodons topple on top of mega vegetation near plasticized hut
□□□□□□)e$_{kl}$ gathering hunters and hunters don't
gather
erotic poetry in a language all tongue
summer for a freedom in time
summer so the freedom is time
ate eat eaten

□□□□□□)e$_{kl}$ + e$_{klm}$(r$_{m}$-□$_{m}$),
s t r e s s
m$_{kl}$ = □□$_{r,r}$ □$_{kl}$ + □□□$_{k,l}$ + □□□$_{l,k}$'
couple stress
in which □$_{kl}$ is the force stress
(which is a symmetric tensor

in classical elasticity but is a s y m m e t r i c h e r e)

out of the can *comes the arrow*

lean meat onto meat

se ep into act ion

per cep tion what a ura p erce ption

gathering happening pride g reat ga me

what unravels the spool from the core

words combine with foliage are foliage

children club the *seals*

children club the *seals*

children club the *seals*

children club the *seals*

ch ild ren club the *s eals*

birds that couldn't fly were clubbed *children* club the *seals*

m_{kl} is the couple stress (or

a fence around the nuclear facility looked n*ice* actually

there was a supermarket selling the red fatty meat of whale

freeze dried a decade ago to eat it is to eat it is and mountains,

erasures

causerie radical interlocution

cumulus clouds fatal

a radioactive map of the brain

they want to perceive the se tting s un

juicy larvae reveal their flavors

more succulent than beetle brittle

an aftermath of attack

killed as a symbol, the remaining, depressed

to be in love, empathy

varying capacities, seasonal

epilogue and legacy despicable john cotton and ilk

cursive despicable legal legal is his song in choir minister (ad)

the right to conquest is written in hefty books prayers players

choose pettycoated coddling grief

acting as beholden

swollen on historical precedent
soiling soil with possession as cult
ure
husb
andry
he's just one *un* culprit
genesis has eaten has eaten **m mm m m**
a strain to envelop alligator through the
jaw that's hinged torpor or whisper
dazed bones thank you
garish gardenish ambience not, but silence (ing ing)
remorse so ever-present eventual like time like lakes like ice
demise dismissed missed moiled re-enterprised loveliness does not
apply
false departure from geo

GRAPHICFORMECOLOGICALFORM

CRESTFALLEN BIODYNAMIC CORE

DREAMTIME FANTASIES ROOTING

OBLIGATORY MORTUARY MIRROR

TOWARD AND AWAY FROM
COMPLICATED LEGACY

UNDERBRUSH OVERRIDE

SEMIOSIS AWAKE UP CALL

SPINAL CORE MULTINATURALLY

now that we have met crawling,

poverty so there's **only** **only** and then s*ome* *only*

w o w t o h a v e a l e g
w o e w e g o f r o m f r o n t l i n e s , d o g g e d w h a t n o t

poverty and duress so home**lessness**

dust attacks **our eyes**
electricity and trophy, butter in the vortex, biodegradable
sort of
a mission for apples appellations
acquires milk from seashore sensor, sand stone dunes
what will go from here, world outside iron oxide
below appellations apparently apparition
peculium with dirt

molecular **disturbance** **breach** stories
altered selves
one is an onion
jejuna & jejune
thee & thine
roisterous
bulked up
bigger

fed them fed them loved them
fed them loved them fed them
fed them held them
captive
fed them loved them
ate them
fed them held them
captive
held them injected them
skinned them
fed them loved them
chained them
harmed them bred them
photographed them housed them
marveled at them
failed to learn their language
fucked them
fucked that we fucked
them up
fucked that that fuck up totalized
in other words this fuck up
fucked all of us up
we are fed up we are closed up we are photographed
brains perform a double description
in the hallway of life
live feed
life feeding
fast forward fasting
an open whole a shut hole
wholly oiled

swimming, burrowing and jumping snakes, all that remains is for us to discover a flying snake

engelmann/obst, *snakes*

with a black snake's un-
winking eye
thinking thinking through glass
through quartz
kamau brathwaite, "ananse"

she ———— *inclined* ————

———— *dissuaded* ————

paste

the beep of insects
the hoo-hoo of bullfrogs
and the croak of toads
companion of a night
when nightmares burgle our sleep.
ken saro-wiwa, "night time"

shore liquid ———— gush turbulent waves ————

———— a speaker ———— speaks

———— ooze ———— water

to swell, wash ——shall

shoal, she'll, hall, shall ________________________________ always some woman
being kept in a cellar
in quoting we track our dirt through the archive
intertwine a manifold engine of cognition
spin an animal ecology of fiber + gel
interpenetrate the gravel of culture
cultural domain desert and grassland
in bondage
and the legacy is a hologramatic cacophony
they have chains around their ankles and wrists
multifocal point of pain
we owe our collective memories
debt management slurping sugar ooze
no choice but to bite the production model that bleeds

shoal, she'll, shall jowl
cannibal, jowl

where the meat stood on a silver platter
w h e e l c h a i r   g l i t t e r e d   o f   b l i n g
in the museum we marveled at the stuffed cats

the museum presents the

beasts as digits

pristis
aspidochelone
fastitocalon
zaratan
jasconius

hafgufa
lyngbakr
great a'tuin
what's standing
right there, left standing stand of trees
the stance and —standability understanding
try as you may it won't grow back, fuck,
f u c k i n g h e l l
u n d e r o r a b o v e e n d i n g
l i k e n i n g a n d e n d s
s h o t p u t b a d l a n d s n i p p e t
i n p u t o u t l y i n g r i p t i d e
a s i n s u l a r a g g r a v a t e d n e c e s s i t y
c a t c h c a n c a n n o t s c a n s i o n
you will be swept away—
primal eyed indeterminacy traversing
an imaginative response (to) (at) the fox farm
red ink as authentic human encounter
bodies were swept away sludge debris silt
something cryptic about the shark (talk)

stand up, st*and* by
however slow is history—by
the children of the stones.
n i z a r q a b b a n i

what cracked open crackpot

longitude

punitive day quotidian

econom

ic like

econom

econom order of

electri

duty

ic like

ic like an

an c order of

chair order of electri

duty electri duty

c

c

chair

chair chinchilla

fur

glands

monogram of fangs
gnaw the surface dimension
where footsteps go obsolete
admixture hot treasure marker

epidermis 

so many alarm calls when to jump, jump
the delight of editing the body as fog takes over electric barking a-
ttributed to humans cooing a-ttributed to humans then we
human s or lowing meaningfully as gravity

seeks remission try to find 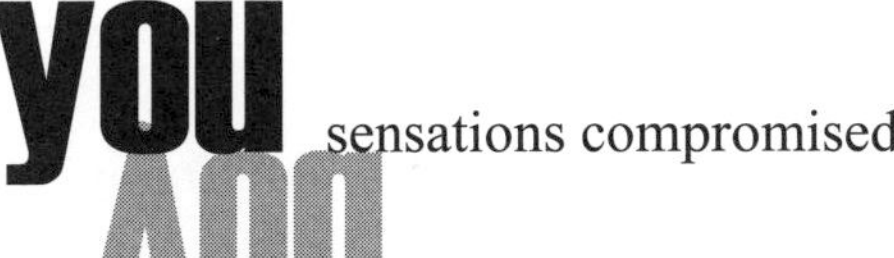

sensations compromised

in the tactile air stacked with rank toxicity still still your
body is the interplay **YOUR BODY**

host to numerous-ity i imagine pointedly a pockmarked desert
body deserted if you were to soldier a-ttributed to gun fire a-tt-
a-ttributed to moats or bridges glow of generation generatively
mirror-osity manifestly we prevent industry from finding us by a
scintillating spiral that sings of succession

later letdown the animal
time and time again

the animal letdown
denaturalized so it seems just you and me

catlike congruity
what does spatiality mean

meat
rights

to call this war a clearing (sing off) (tender to remove thread) (full inside) (insidious)
the days seem spooled (with empathy) (vision throngs) (deliverance

on the level of a nano model)

her (because of) splendor (ardor) resiliencies (risk)

look (become) see (the hosts) we wend

to say kinship alters touch (do) (that) (thanos)

immediate density (fit) and (fits) (doing done value work)

biological headdress (nudity?) (body melded) (sake)

infra (structure) (i) deology (i'd) cope (cap) able (to) day

ax specific

REMEMBERING

you, animal

bird (no) (bird) oh
og (d) took me for a w (alk) oh
we used his d (og's) (le(ash) ou (y) wouldn't beli(eve)
ood(f) from the hu(man) b(owl) tasted foul blo(odd) g(round)d(own)
b(ones) waste susp(ended) in jell(y smelly) is canned is what we are
served to survive
soylent of green is what i mean
at(e) e(m) and you'll die in(sect)icide
aggregates insoluble inside insect gut
press upon you meaning of dog
meaning of me(at) dog

city of cells we welled up site for service
measure turgidity
we welt oh well deep as black wasser
political insect kennel castle-fix
hydrogenated canine lab top diet
aibo ought to bite you
bred to be sacrificed when the price is right
enlivening polyester bubble forms
fake fur delicatessen
lionize the elk
the elk (!) once alpine peaks are reconditioned

kitten squalor (sealed into rooms) puppy pulp
make sure every species is in stock
poodles wearing crowns are regal
dispose beaks with each pecking order
lame duck on the lamb
tame all mortal fiber with geodesic imaginings
yes, *affirmed for sacrifice*
your lamb, sheep, goat, ram, cow, bull, rabbit
irony in the heel of a sow
kitten can't contend or can contend *when venturing out of*
wooded scenarios a topical scene two dimensional
crystal prisms catchy at window prompt for outer world
containment on a ship where crumbled iron gleams
what is hidden and riding on iron beneath the balustrade
desires coiled like exotica making way to shore
hawaii will have these snakes brown like twine with vital hunger
on london plane trees before this bed are glistening beetles boring
topical holes spraying agencies come by and treat bark with liquid
attack i watch as the tree struggles neighbors despise all growth
sweating ice is my imagination's outlet

to show affection——used especially <u>of a dog</u> _________

            <u>court the cat</u>__________   cringing
used <u>especially of a dog</u> _______________polis truckling as many
as there are, each and every treeless occasion oxygenation
as many as there are, birds
vulture justice
                        in your chicken suit and pork pie hat
harlequin road runner   ma roadrunner wile e. coyote
don’t take kindly to that

(proliferation of dog breeds in victorian times when leisure meant
you needed a pet, “sit!” “down!” “fetch!” “good boy”)
concusses effigies sit tight sit lean
lean in learn **LEARN** lure alluring

a body that offers space (in competition) with bodies
grow onto growth
body without eyes softly illegible a wild mirror
pleasure seeking fur coat coats

said to be your best friend
on command
privileged by a living room sofa
difficulty in being
property of

poodle <u>preen</u>

chihuahua <u>hardship</u>

<u>chicken in/chicken out=over and out</u>

specimens in a holding tank

own the debt pelt

especially of a dog

i was invented for my plastic spine, convertible features
stuffed up, scanty, with air
water is evocative
history, the result of voice
the difficulty i have is writing mother
dogs understand (me) best
a whale bone corset holds passion wailing

her poem:

by the sock monkey bureau
sewn up at the eyes
stuffed in the mouth

…heather fuller's poem:

she kept worrying til she wore clean through
cartilage bathed in broken bottle disembodied
bit off their heads and weeds grow horizontal

scandal at waters

+ didn't know how to proceed with the (rotting arm) (indenturing)
a country road that led to utopia, ha the outer galaxy here
gun of difficulty   got
tires burning under venus' light
claims a woman's privilege is dark is dark
a voice (ours) said united as (horror)
scantily country fed with disgust
pigs we ate were missing limbs
depressed meat kneeling
watch her mother feed
the map gives some idea where the suture serves
to be sarcasm at the chain-linked noose
one downed to go
the glowing cages thick with heat are chicks breeding for slaughter
to supposedly be a chick   (en) (en) (en)
there are pits thick with black and get harvested as work
with this fuel a book is read the engine cranks life support
gurgles
she and i look for beauty in the nakedness of fright
or the beauty manifested in some continuum thrum
the beauty so thickly embezzled
so snarled
a sarcasm scarcasm

note to selves about nut:
for sky and heavens, mother and guardian, demi-animals,
immortality, physical prowess
totemic form: cow
said in pig latin

ra asked nut to raise him into the heavens to remove him from the world, which he found distasteful. carrying him on her back, nut rose upward, but the higher she reached, the dizzier she became. she would have crashed to the ground if four gods had not steadied her legs and while shu held up her belly. these gods became the four pillars of the sky, and nut's body became the firmament, to which ra attached the stars.

to be portrayed
either as a lion or a woman
and seem to enjoy killing
fire vengeance
beer in the case of sekhmet
curbed the killing of the human race

HISTORICAL PHASE

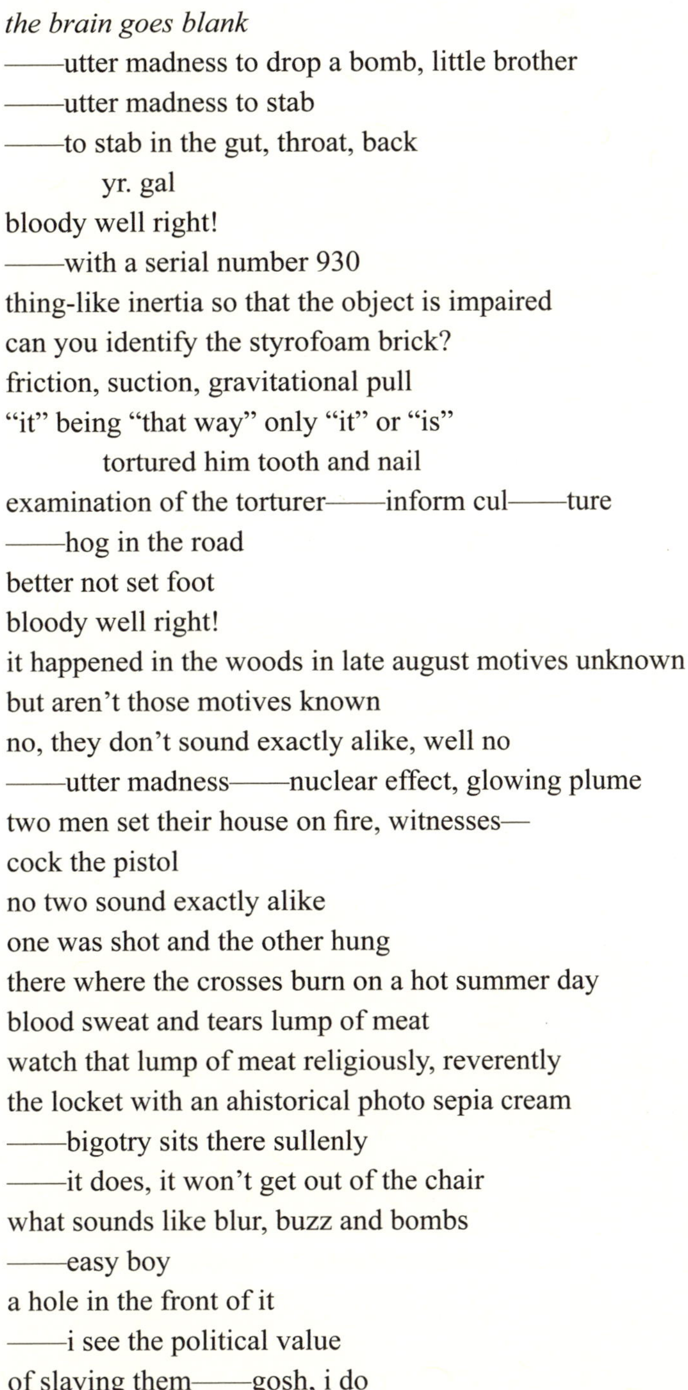

the brain goes blank
——utter madness to drop a bomb, little brother
——utter madness to stab
——to stab in the gut, throat, back
yr. gal
bloody well right!
——with a serial number 930
thing-like inertia so that the object is impaired
can you identify the styrofoam brick?
friction, suction, gravitational pull
"it" being "that way" only "it" or "is"
tortured him tooth and nail
examination of the torturer——inform cul——ture
——hog in the road
better not set foot
bloody well right!
it happened in the woods in late august motives unknown
but aren't those motives known
no, they don't sound exactly alike, well no
——utter madness——nuclear effect, glowing plume
two men set their house on fire, witnesses—
cock the pistol
no two sound exactly alike
one was shot and the other hung
there where the crosses burn on a hot summer day
blood sweat and tears lump of meat
watch that lump of meat religiously, reverently
the locket with an ahistorical photo sepia cream
——bigotry sits there sullenly
——it does, it won't get out of the chair
what sounds like blur, buzz and bombs
——easy boy
a hole in the front of it
——i see the political value
of slaying them——gosh, i do

when it comes to honor and inalienable rights backstabbing
the way things are done around here you hear
a little fox hunting——biological essentialism
watch the animals die…
…it is incumbent upon us
"that" being "this way" sway
a legacy, the way it pertains to
the relatively huge brain of the whale
on the fourth of july——cobra helicopter
the bat's sonar capacities——cobra helicopter——cobra
helicopter——unstated proviso
till the backyard glows with torpor
till there is (theirs-whose) fear (these) in every blade of grass
countervailed by the garden
the history that rises up from the lawn
self-determination and a fence as was seen
report what's hot:

"gripped by a 10th straight day of 100-degree heat, california sweated out the possibility of more blackouts yesterday as the number of suspected heat-related deaths climbed to at least 38 and the rotting carcasses of thousands of dairy cows and other livestock baked in the sun" *am ny,* issue #140, volume 4, wednesday, july 26th, 2006

:

that politician vowed to kill off additional species

    and

that politician pledged to increase fossil fuel emissions

    and that little politician ran

that little politician ran——and sure enough,
ate roast beef, as did another little politician, ate roast beef
as the saying goes: eat roast beef

that little piggy had none

steel, grp composites, glass, pig and formaldehyde solution, electric
motor, glass tanks

fufio-caninian law 2 bc *petrographic*

42° 41' 38" N, 73° 6' 54" W (42.693899, -73.115096) GR1

there, 18.2% live under the poverty line (2000 census)

FAILED A SIGNAL

28-year old sandra bland
is pulled over by state trooper
brian encinia for “failing to signal
a lane change”
step out of the car
i will remove you
get out, NOW
GET OUT OF THE CAR
I WILL LIGHT YOU UP
he has his taser pointed at her
officer brian encinia’s dash cam
continues to
document the
i think i know you, but are you real
are you really you
she had gotten a new job
and was excited about it
he put her in handcuffs
and forced her to the ground
waller county jail
bland was booked
for third-degree
felony and was placed
alone in a cell that
typically accommodates
four inmates, authorities said
the last time sandra bland
is seen alive is at
7 a.m on
monday, july 13
if sandra bland did not
do this to herself
someone else did
this to her

HUMAN HOLOGRAM

We are all sensitive people
with their chokeholds + shoot first ask later protocols
with their plywood covered watchtowers
with their perspex riot shields
with their fortifications + reinforcements
with their restrictive arc around us
with their mediated outcomes
with their supremacism hatred-ideology
deployed tear gas and smoke bombs on us
deployed military grade apparatus on us
deployed tanks on us
deployed curfews on us
deployed dogs on us
deployed rubber bullets and pepper spray on us
deployed electroshock, sonic and ultrasonic canons
deployed extra-aural bioeffects
deployed SWAT teams on us
the trajectory the timeline takes
circulation of power and energy
turfing intensity
tracking the mood
tracking the mode
we will make rid of the tyrannical father
we will dissolve the glass monoliths
we will repudiate capital
we will eradicate the industrial, military, prison, complex
we will disavow brutality
we are sensitive to the epigenetic condition
we are responsive to healing
we initiate the pivoting of senses
a relational dynamic of skin and fire
confrontation of metal and sign

LIP SERVICE

we've come a long way from the upper limbs of trees
we've come a long way from the dismal swamps
we've come a long way from the clear-cut forest
we've come a long way from the prison leasing system
we've come a long way from the feeding lots
we've come a long way from the vivisections
we've come a long way from internecine battles
we've come a long way from apartheid segregation
we've come a long way from trigger ready landmine mega bombs
we've come a long way from the penitentiaries for the insane
we've come a long way from the toxic laden clouds
we've come a long way from utopian desire
we've come a long way from redress
we are heading towards the future as if it was universal principle
we are heading toward death as if death was a reckoning
we are heading toward timelessness as if in a line
we are treading in place within metaphorical language
we are trending towards extinction models with all other animals
we are blending with the foliage as ice caps are melting
we are making more holding tanks for the people we fear
we are making more molds for the objects that we trash
we are making more chemicals for the processes we wish for
we've discovered a way to outsize war and perpetuate grief
we've discovered a way to genetically modify life
we've discovered a way to map the outer galaxies
we've perfected a way to record our every gesture
we've perfected the means to harness memory
microbiopolitics nuzzle our wholesome
economic collapse glorifies our gardens
amid imaginings of catastrophic possible futures worlds unfold
strategies of reciprocity weaken hegemonies
time is a massive hologram
dogmas crowd our ecological living room
we once were animals and now we are animals

TRAGEDY (VISIBLE, SEMI-VISIBLE, UNBEKNOWNST TO THE ENCULTURATED EYE + WHAT OF NIGHTLY TV)

tall chrome modern waterfall
faucet

list price: ~~$499.99~~
today's price: $229.99

"what is skunk spray israel uses against palestinians?"

"stood at the polling station wearing a sandwich board for most of the day"

"accent any room—but hurry, the savings won't last…"

"ISIL fights syrian rebels near aleppo as army prepares assault"

"study finds climate change as threat to 1 in 6 species"

"…she is in a welfare-to-work program, making fudge for rich people in the suburbs…"

"we are always in the comfort zone—see about lease offers…"

"you will hear from a mom who was bitten by a snake"

"an abrupt climate change scenario and its implications for united states national security"

"it touched every american—this was truly a tragic assault"

"bring more to the table in only 90 seconds"

"...from the creator of the *quattro*"

"...32 caliber...bleeding into bleeding..."

"he has to pay $15,000 a month for child support"

"graphic video shows college student who died in custody was tased in restraint chair"

"how much profit is enough, we tried to dial in the
subsidies..."

"euphoria by calvin klein—live the dream"

"glad—force flex—for stretchable hold—get glad"

"question: when is shooting a 12-year-old child reasonable?

"edward snowden and black lives matter activist deray mckesson had a great dialogue about surveillance"

we are here/here amongst us... *grrrrr*

talk around the obvious. the whole country's going to shit. &
you too. & me. a street. stuffed with flowers.
warehouses of scents. dog doo on the path.
a man cries dry coughs.
let's go for a field trip kiddies up up & away. the cow.
was it the cow. was it a moon. prostitute.
caught up in a groove.
repeat offenders. jump. yeah. keep time.
AKILAH OLIVER, *she said, let the little squeals assemble*

children's animal chair - zebra (colombia)

list price:	~~$74.99~~
today's price:	$39.99
you save:	$35.00 (46%)
catalog #:	10018127

33 million people are uprooted by war…entire generations of people have grown up as refugees or internally displaced people (idps). more than 2 million afghans living in iran and pakistan, and more that 400,000 sudanese living in various neighboring countries have stayed in camps and other temporary shelters for more than 20 years. more than 2 million palestinians have been displaced for up to 57 years… www.doctorswithoutborders.org

dystopian pleasuredome

settler theme park

survivalville

punishment garden

factory farm prison oblivion chamber

humanized animal habitat

be prepared to be bombed back into the stone ages... our own g.w. bush to pakistan's president pervez musharraf

pakistan's president pervez musharraf has rejected accusations he is a western "poodle," saying his fight against islamic militants is for his country's benefit, not for the united states or britain.

"i am nobody's poodle," he said in an interview with britain's guardian newspaper on friday. "i have enough strength of my own to lead."

robotic blissdome

sticker price labor gratification bubble

zero feedback loop continuity parlor

resource mongering judicial palace

curative rescue fantasy

futuristic meltdown feather puff help site

spider hole/eagle's nest

IN THE SOUTH OF GERMANY, VERY HIGH LEVELS OF CESIUM IN THE SOIL PERSISTS; HUNTERS ARE COMPENSATED FOR CATCHING CONTAMINATED ANIMALS, AND MANY MUSHROOMS AND WILD BERRIES ARE STILL TOO RADIOACTIVE TO EAT.
HELEN CALDICOTT, *NUCLEAR POWER IS NOT THE ANSWER*

grandiose narcissism restorative facility

pseudo forest young white lad retreat

future ruler prep school

menagerie bestiary trophy wife powder room

topical black bloc arrest station

happy hour three step program

as for *akōn*, as louis gernet pointed out, it associates all kinds of ideas that, from the point of view of psychology, should be carefully distinguished right from the start. the single expression of *phonos akousios*, referring to the murder committed despite oneself, can mean now a total absence of guilt, now mere negligence, now a positive lack of prudence, now even a more or less fleeting impulse or the quite different case of homicide committed in legitimate self-defense. the fact is that the hek*ōn-akōn* opposition is not the fruit of disinterested reflection on the subjective conditions that make an individual the cause responsible for his actions. it is rather a matter of legal categories that, at the time of the city-state, were imposed by the law as norms for common thought. now the law did not proceed on the basis of a psychological analysis of the varying degrees of the responsibility of the agent. it followed criteria designed to regulate, in the name of the state, the exercise of private vengeance, by drawing distinctions, in accordance with the varying intensity of emotion reaction aroused in the group in question, between the various forms of murder calling for different legal sentences.

jean-pierre vernant and pierre vidal-naquet, *myth and tragedy in ancient* greece

elite security surveillance gated community hedgework

normative elementary school shooting session lunch break

wide-eyed mascaraed anorexic runaway age-defying strobelight

fema camp wide screen tv downtime

cradle to grave debt pool with 100 chippendales lifeguards

wall street billionaire sweepstakes giveaway

there is blood in my owl vagina blood in my alma soul blood on the opening in the earth bright ruby crust. there is blood all over that land does god have the vapors i ask the american secretary of state does alma our god. i study the coupling patterns of blood on the napkin of the maddened woman, the beginning of a massive period of blood implying mother black red and rubied, the shadows of the blood compel me to speak in the voice of the earth.

alice notley *alma or the dead woman*

racial discriminatory discount big box shop till you drop going once sale

prismatic kaleidoscopic secret rendition site

wondrous peaks and valleys smog choked fracked reservoir

two crisis' for one blue light special

paramilitary proxy war with cream on top

death of ocean fantasy reality

the erewhonians regard death with less abhorrence than disease. if it is an offence at all, it is one beyond the reach of the law, which is therefore silent on the subject; but they insist that the greater number of those who are commonly said to die, have never yet been born— not, at least, into that unseen world which is alone worthy of consideration. as regards this unseen world I understand them to say that some miscarry in respect to it before they have even reached the seen, and some after, while few are ever truly born into it at all—the greater part of all the men and women over the whole country miscarrying before they reach it. and they say that this does not matter so much as we think it does.

samuel butler, *chapter XIII: the views of the erewhonians concerning death*

saw-see-seeing-seen

punitive paradise

debunked dunked waterboarded swoon bunker

rarified rape tableau mansion

super smart hurt art bastion

consented endorsed ideologically beautiful mountain

chivalrous pop patriarchal primal cell

alarmed by the data that showed trace levels of pharmaceuticals in european streams, researchers in the united states have begun to survey our nation's waterways. in 2002, the usgs published the results of its first-ever reconnaissance of man-made contaminants. using highly sensitive assays, the agency found traces of 82 different organic contaminants—fertilizers and flame retardants as well as pharmaceuticals—in surface waters across the nation. these drugs included natural and synthetic hormones, antibiotics, anti-hypertensives, painkillers, and antidepressants. elizabeth royte, *drugging the waters* in *onearth*

foregone conclusionary hiatus think tank

calcified mortuary sweet scented death trap

selfie animal trope please feed me motif

you walk here I walk there activist movement

strength of the male governing voiceless retreat

war atrocity addled spiritual journey

grip 10-piece women's tool kit

list Price: ~~$94.99~~

today's price: $29.99

you save: $65.00 (68%)

catalog #: 10307150

quantity:

1

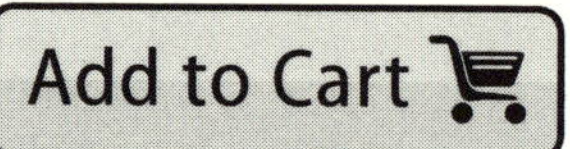

You can remove item later if you'd like.

CRY I

Four moths, thuringia

resistance developed quickly eaten fields of vapor
skyhold no clouds thrashing blinding sunscape
nope, sun
epithelial cells have lyse d release d un of s
gut cell membrane so when it licks it sickens sun
sun when opening pathogen binding affinities
control screen with ravens set sun sun
oon-m noon sun

at(e) e(m) and you'll die in(sect)icide

black fly vector *hector* *horus* so(s)

solubilized in eyes our eyes in vectors suns

i bore a black beetle active

sun, i wore helmet membranes skin wings antennae

un, i gore (s) abhor where once noose

animal, you've

phase whore boy your disparagement alpha helices [places]

sunscreen i mean mean [detrimental, mental, ‘mean’]

[cede] pregnancy bait wait pleasure gut cellular

wingless raven welter vector   sun [screens]

i mean i mean i’m a combination

larvae stopped feeding/host gut/tremor

breathing machines form in embryonic fluid, body be (fore)
circumstance glances whor-ses *horses* horses
we bet on the plumb winning torso
hooves index a circular track
when they’ll race you naked on the cul-de-sac
insects cheer at your success

liquid replicas

living cells are motives like color
to mirror your meat perception
jewelry and volume and canyon
inkling overlaps in image
"a creature"

                    a jpeg the transgenetic cactus
(that she engineered, considers art), it sprouts human hair

there's a hare named bunny (and it)
glows phosphorescent green

art envisions

what art envisions

tip a cell *this way*

REMIX RIVER STYX BY HOMETOWN HARDCORE DAVID RANDALL

i'll have my ham with spam and jam.

it will make me what i am. i am.

television is my library, and depth is only screen deep.

leap from a jeep while contemplating advertising the hunting of something rare.

like my ham which fills me and make me ill.

i read your words, the herds or words and they trampled me.

i ate the ham between two slices of cheetah.

i wonder why the sudanese have 100 thousand chinese soldiers, oil untapped
and,   our "we" creating refugees.

and slaves sold by the masters of us all.

? we'll *rescue them* for the oil—
what do the cheetahs have? will the
chinese fight to keep the cheetahs—usa? or will they have ham in a slammer and
myself while i am.

i only know what they told me and i know what they didn't say. when it's
all said and done, where will the cheetahs play? will they? will they be?
or will they be just that much more ham or spam for those who say i am.

skip the ham. i'll just have jam, because economic slaves can never say i am.

CRY II

$\sigma_{kl} = \lambda e_{rr}\, \delta_{kl} + (2\,\mu + \kappa\,)e_{kl} + e_{klm}(r_m - \phi_m)$, ***stress***
$m_{kl} = \alpha_{\ r,r}\, \delta_{kl} + \beta\, \phi_{k,l} + \gamma\, \phi_{l,k}$, ***couple stress***

the free energy density for general anisotropy is

$\Psi = A_{\ 0} + A_{\ kl}\varepsilon_{kl} + (1/2)A_{\ klmn}\varepsilon_{kl}\,\varepsilon_{mn} + B_{\ kl}\phi_{k,l} +$
$(1/2)B_{\ klmn}\phi_{k,l}\phi_{m,n} + C_{\ klmn}\varepsilon_{kl}\phi_{m,n}$,
with $\varepsilon_{kl} = e_{\ kl} + \varepsilon_{klm}(r_m - \phi_m)$.

the ease of collecting bones of the mammoth as the permafrost melts

25,000 year old bones
25,000 year old bones
25,000 year old bones
25,000 year old bones
25,000 year old bones
25,000 year old bones
25,000 year old bones

operation grapes of wrath

argus: inventors work on a model of the snarky dog it'll have a noose chain bling smelling collar noose chain bling throttle collar bark at snark bark will come with sparkling collar snark at demise of shark like bling it shines out loud in the outdoor gallery tree of life donning satellites

the we that is washington

a repellant ***t(cell)*** *hink a very pretty thing*

war related violence in shiite area of baghdad

think, pig (pozzo jerks the rope. lucky looks at pozzo.) think pig!
sheer lancelot volatility

killing 22 people and wounding 28
now that we have met crawling, swimming, burrowing and jumping
snakes, all that remains is for us to discover a flying snake

shiitte corner of dora, a predominant sunni arab district of baghdad

glossy marbleized slabs of ham i am iam

car bomb exploded   rocked almost daily by bombings,
ambushes, assassinations
100 million children or thereabouts
are homeless, sleep on the streets

most vulnerable most in need

________________________________deploy

________offensive huge_______push______convoy_____shelling

_____________________________fresh attack

__________________________die violent deaths

_____catastrophe in our hands

cartilage morsel a neckline flank
through the act of breathing one makes the most of their vessel
lotus position sheerings shimmering as thinking recedes into
thinking
coagulate no end no beginning permutation as a proper name

pleasured by a grove of birch
blood rushed mound   of soil

touch taunt skin sooth epidermal stretch *frémissement cataire*

proportion arable timber district
beautiful continuousness immense presence

it doesn't fit as nicely
as one would hope

pig-a-letto mezzo soprano, bar code on my (m) (heat) a
slaughterhouse to live out the rest of your life
abattoirs
the status of horses in our culture (break spirit, will)

how estrogen is collected for human replenishment/dire. horse's ire

shattered bits of fruit and vegetables from venders' pushcarts lay
scattered on the street amid pools of blood

to put this in writing by the gutter in the sagging flesh

water and sewage infrastructure was promised *promised* to
people water was tainted the environment poisoned museums looted
ravaged a desert storm a desert storm

am that animal culpable i of a collective singularly notwithstanding
time frame era race gender class

anti-personal cluster bombs——katyusha rockets

jus in bello ***jus ad bello***

my lips don't want to get around king's english as in savage
notably as if noble psychopathically or
do i mean systematically
sadistic
savioristic
a toughening expression
a tool that blunts

kallikak kink juke joke

economic like an electric
chair

pitted against other (each)

bravery is a characteristic of this animal

zoonosis

CRY III

one mono culture designed to mitigate the
other

water fowl **one mono culture**
designed to
mitigate the other

cattails
habituated to t—heir miseries
that of the bodies dead—ening/lay strewn about
earthquakes, volcanic eruptions, famines, epidemics
subjugated flesh of victims

marcus aurelius died of pestilence **one**
mono culture
designed to
mitigate the other

"during the whole of lent we ate no fish except eels; and the eels,
which are ravenous feeders, fed on the corpses."
account of the 7th crusade by one john joinville (1224-1318)

one mono culture designed to
mitigate the other

ark
made of gopher wood
red ants
camphor, ether, formaldehyde
of fur, feather

and chitons **one mono culture**
designed to
mitigate the other

the elephant war = sabaeans in yemen
prosperity based on spice, capital ma'rib

HOC ERAT IN VOTIS : A BIT OF LAND

one mono culture designed to mitigate another

trepanned the skulls
trepan the skull

one mono culture designed to
mitigate another

"slavery was begun by the spaniards in 1501 and british participation dated from 1593, with the ships running between angola and the river plate."
j.d. gillett, *the mosquito: its life, activities, and impact on human affairs*

one mono culture

one aspect of war surely must be to render (reduce) the enemy (other) to ugliness. to be hideous, ridiculous, scarred, without full posture of confidence (sunken) see abu ghraib. — abjectness of otherwise beautiful physique — how ugly the soldiers imitating the terror look finally in comparison to the subjugated flesh of victims—then to dehumanize, meaning to render one's humanity null, then we are what, we are what, for the pain for the suffering that is brought to the fore to be removed from contingency suddenly

only the only-ness of the extreme situation dunked into chilling tanks of water submerged until until until then the cage the dank surround the footsteps to render the enemy beyond representation rendition through pain so that the mind must house the body for survival the human trait of intimidation how sensible creatures share this no caveat fool's cap electric shock waiting game torn out torn out extremity heartbeat extremity heartbeat pulse pulse menacing and incoherent unventilated cells with frightening acoustics bang echo pure relationship rod cone rebar hall the outside of concept

designed to mitigate another

at any time

enclosures

then

to deceive you

two jugs of beer

put around her tree

oh hour our never or

i, really i

sit at pine desk————————weep, reap

the hour is lost on a cycle of work

i did not know

————harvested————

was a complete version

sun eclipsed by screens

tender diminutive
from the female
name ekaterina

animal that rhymes with culture

leather, timber
myriads of black crickets
army worms
vine aphid
locust eggs and nymphs
havoc egg: head of cattle, devour, exorcism
assassin bugs

the refugee's description of space

"insects of the order hemiptera are characterized by the possession of sucking mouth-parts enclosed in a segmented beak. these most important from a medical standpoint are the cimicida or bed bugs and the reduviidae or assassin bugs."

this camp

as if war
were a witticism

Pitted
against
each
other

Pitted
against
each
other

Pitted
against
each
other

Pitted
against
each
other

Pitted
against
each
other

Pitted
against
each
other

sarcasm nightfall
terror vestibule
granular slather
gave the impression
compelling news
appendages/prosthetics/extensions

stigmatized

pitfall greasemonkey erasure ₪ chatzilla, teen communities bud ₪ bug 337095 on the object of knowledge tree there beyond the trusted window ₪ search as they do for documentation daemons take root ₪ debugger thunderbird ₪ authenticate your name starbird sunbird mostly crystal hylic ₪ protoplasm seamonkey build your domain ₪ login login seamonkey ₪ code snippets mostly crystal

corpus → body extends itself through history, gonads,
dispersions of particularized info atomized. reconciliation through
modes of pixilation. grit-posit-ive. live. cell-phonetics.
wrangle-ation. hook-n-bait mechanism get-what-you-want
emporium, commence in domination aspersion incursion hellion, in
case of evacuation your fellow man. fat not that dot could be
explosion, planetary delirium. a bridge, night fall
urgency to fade.
don't you know me, oh eyes. crises
crisis. down to earth.
downed. then some. blossoming.
immense spawning, variegated proliferations

was entirely different

wolf spider/stag beetle
sarcasm nightfall
witticism,
feeding on mammal blood
spilled much money **refugees**
they were
rotting, like body (a) carbon her my hair remained in clumps

an ethnic difference and the architecture

family, my brothers——weep

a direct result——an unknowable

difference, explanation

language that encloses such horror

our heads
father, four children
known as civilians
dead under ruins
10-15 days
metabolically
cars stacked up
fleeing

bombing strikes

hot smashed

could not carry their worldly goods with them

tyre and then shifts in space, shifts in space

the elephant war

extol/repel a barbed wire fence hence
hence equally valid
partially inclusive
overlapping
whole of ecologies
biomes
organisms contained
find you you you in continuum we we we are are you with you

one mono culture designed to
mitigate the other

blur buzz, bombs
malingering
racism, the hatred caused by capital its lack its hollowing
out hate sister hate brother mother father
territory————————terror

one mono culture designed to
mitigate another

ideological straightjacket, cuff link plus fence

one mono culture designed to
mitigate another

firsthand account neck account spinal account

one mono culture designed to
mitigate the other

for ***claudette colvin***

for ***ida b. wells***

for ***marie w. stewart***

for ***aurelia browder***

for ***irene morgan***

for ***jo ann gibson robinson***

for ***viola gregg liuzzo***

for ***katie wingfield***

for ***geneva johnson***

for ***mary fair burks***

for ***mary church terrell***

for ***mary louise smith***

for ***rosa parks***

TESTIFY, BEAR WITNESS, EXHORT, ANNOTATE, COMPEL, CONFRONT, SPEAK, APPROVE OR OTHERWISE COMMENT ON— — — DURATIVE MODE OF "TO BE"

CRY IV

"the general followed the step brothers, having been introduced by co-chairman pearson. "people say it's foolish to send all those turkeys to mississippi, when the people don't have anything to cook them on. when the ku klux klan hears what we're up to, they'll burn enough crosses to roast an elephant. anyway, they can just break off a frozen wing and have a turksicle."

introduction to dick gregory's, *shadow that scares me* by reverend james r. mcgraw

extremity——animosity

rotten which bleached
shows we—a— we
————worst/worsted

moo o o o o   "too dog"

ra b i t ra bit

r a b i t r a bi t   DO YOU MEAN "RABBIT" ?
r a bi t r a b i t

————swoosh   "state bird"

tr uck ish
  (f)
tru cks or
cars is(f)
fis h es ary

such scary peopling

a gathering such as a picnic

all morally righteous

strange sociality

super strange

what were they

doing on such a

fine, fine day

?

??????????????????????
???
????????????????????????????????????? ???????????????
???????????? ???????????????????
??
??????????????? ??????????????????? ?????????????
??
???????? ??
?????????????????????????????? ????????????????????????????????
??????????????????????????????? ?????????????????????????
???????? ???
???
?? ???????????
?????????????????????????????? ????????????????????????? ???
???
???????????? ??????????????? ?????????????????????????
?????????????????????????????????

counterpoint to gas mask cat
de   cap   it   ated
rat   bird
of   prey
elephant————emotional

hormonal meat

equine anatomical————

"the dog who shits…the song of the flesh"

altruistic chicken little species nirvana

photomontage, gulch, with inscription, glued
carcass difficult   neo squid super conducting quantum
interference device   relative cheap, crude
splintered speech not a juridical invention
what was your innovation
how does it serve your nation
what sort of insulation | presences | **insults** | **salutations**

inside our minds a mortuary

an extinction event beyond the pale

herald in an era of scarcity

animals are going

this is a stress test

neo SquiD

WALLABIES

horse, he's sick

cut and past

horse race

ova

jowl

jawline

leg brace

TREE KANGAROO

bhopal/carbide we are wrong we wronged
rung of ladder lung of matter

responsible agents float fascinate how teeth fly
how loftily does each signifier
floats flaunts flees
heart grows in turkey
distended arm sheep
frog didacticism repeat: the vein
swan and devil
skeletal claim
eviscerated no doubt about it rope

use a female nude as usual

she gentle sexual
she aggressive bold commandeered took made is
made use of hook

wand
siphon

wounded suggests lungs

calls to mind

social expectations of the bones
impaired role

medical erotic wounded

**the methods of torture include the
pau de arara (parrot's perch)
setting fire to parts of the body
which have been dampened with
alcohol, injection of ether under the
skin, strong electric shocks and...**

nancy spero, *torture of women*

worn stained torn seeping

behind cabinet nematode

men's arms——
central motif rattle

chimera splice

cost of young boy as it pertains to flora

vestige

make sure waste blessing coast biogeneticists
have found that human ritual is "both inescapably enculturated and biogenetically
controlled" (mitchell 1993:43)

The entire contents of the monkey outfit are:

1 X RED CLOAK

1 X GREY TROUSERS

1 X GOLD NECKERCHIEF

1 X PAIR BOOTS SIZE 8 -10

1 X LEATHER BELT

1 X GOLD HEADBAND

1 X WIG

1 X PAIR SIDE BURNS

1 X PAIR EYEBROWS

1 X BLACKEYELINER

1 X MAKE UP GLUE FOR SIDE BURNS ETC

1 X STAFF

sexualized to the point of in-
finity

nice shit hole
foxy
vixen

coldness: noted for her sexual appeal
peeling skin apples
ball of twine
reptilian brain
ready-made sugar cube
allusive
coldness
half effaced perfectionist light bulb
contains aura

zebra caterpillar
zebra wolf
zebra spider
zebra shark
zebra swallowtail
zebra parakeet
zebra conniption

wooden creature regionally expressed in
autobiographic shorthand when you open this book to the
prairie the arctic circle
as if it were a portal
trading furs `serious exhortation to the`
`inhabitants of that land` `reparations`
likely/unlikely

it'll soon ensue

IT'LL SOON ENSUE: VOLATILIZATION

shell shocked pink tribe-i'd, you'd
globe babe——grave——yard, fess
confession

play dead does play

sick cuz
white elephant trigonometry
ai, bot or vec
transhuman/infrahuman

sicker yet

giraffe

will fetch death
hoove
you wait and be

don't be shy wait moon
stroke it pet

silly cuz your skeleton

dome litter esque

boring   (the)   meat

ham   burger (helper)
portrait   class
depiction song
hot dog   song

subjugation bubbles the tropes

festival where we enter the pig
rollick spore
mental health of the whales, boars
petting zoo, the menagerie, animal magazine

depicted [worst] attribute
   fierce
      flesh eating: man
eating
   as if
   dirty quick
   sultry dense
squirrely   shown as monkey freak
slime
hemoglobin
shown rash blob butter ‘er up blandish
saucy   blanched moist

CRY V

aamzamaz: *bowels of a lamb* chick: what does this make you think——of

mule: *bag l* *scapegoat*
cow: bagra

butcher: *bouci* prefers barren areas with few trees, mountain steepes, and high plateaus feeds on bodies left on funeral pyres sie prefers the tundra

lamb's brain: bouzellouf
buca ecaae: *stork*

ADOPTION AND CONCEPTS OF MISCEGENATION

djaad: *chicken* *idiot, fool*: djaayeh

pig: out, pig out du uda: *worm*
fermented walrus: tuktaq cat: cat's meow
normative features thrust
qaquablaabnaqtuq: is tense because of impending unpleasantness earth like lost wax, the fear of pointing at space, seamless parting curtains, we are being displaced, there is little ice, our livelihood, under duress, sivuniqtuuguuruq: is obstinate, listening ears tuned off sivunniqsuq: decides, plans

sitquaq: *rear flipper of a seal*

manned by snake blood/camel hump, hunch, haunch

of a sea mammal whose body curves high out of
water: muqpaktuq

sluggish

qiviuq down: *of water fowl, wool of musk ox*

crept along on muscular feet
chitons eat algae, bryozoans, diatoms and occasionally
bacteria by scraping the rocky substrate with their well-
developed radula, beautiful rough tongues

ukpiqtuaguqatisi: your fellow believers, reap what you sow reap what you know images turn red sun turns blue shout of a language last to leave lasting in her heart how does time appear in puzzled human dawn

siqijhatittuq: *slaps the water with its tail;*
beaver

spanish moth

qavaqtug: *sleeps on its back in water; seal*

water (undrinkable): imaq
imiq: *water (drinkable)*

ice: there are less than 900 polar bears in
existence what does this make you think of

nimibiaq: *water worm, eel, serpent, snake*

imavaalua: *water's sound*

groan: imeiqsaktug

built of grass, twigs and excrement

WE'VE NEVER VENTURED THERE

imaqsirug: *moisten skin*

whines (dog) (human): imfaluktuq

half-black person: taaqsipaiyaaq
half-white person: tania yaaq

piyaqqubvik: *place of accident*

red herrings drones feed baby
with royal jelly: queen
down there, down river, ocean

STATUS QUO HOME TOWN CULTURE
HUMANS ARE SUSCEPTIBLE OF BEING
CAUGHT UP BY THE NEXT NEW THING
beast entomology
THING HYBRIDIZED, HAS MULTIPLE
ORIGINS, MAYBE BONOBO, MAYBE
FINCH, GOAT'S BEARD, POLYPLOIDY

opisthokonts where to shit, fuck, sleep———the shit
loads of garbage sent in a barge down river or pay off another
country to take
we (humans) are the sister group of
the choanoflagellates
cihuacoatl was a fierce goddess and
an omen…by night she walked
weeping
wailing; also an omen of war
cross-modal transfer: hello, innervations from the brain to the larynx—caterpillars
king kong disney-fied big
mice
mummies kaapa
when neck is stretched out pig out the word that
the brain focuses on: natural, naturalistic—complex motor tendencies
prehominid days
cricket moving van
pretext for aggression

anthropod vector "in the evolutionary perspective, then, society and genetic programming imply each other."
mary midgley, from *beast and man*

cochineal insects "foul owl on the prowl"

hyracotherium [eohippus] ssp., the dog-sized ancestors of the horse

what is the nature of the question

troödon-descended sapient

rib cage, cortex, thorax

epidemiological data tankers

see how shamo makes his living

CHLOROFLOROCARBONS

spring hill mine disaster crop that top of hill

bertolt brecht, saint joan of the stockyards

"similarly, storm-water runoff from urban areas may contain large amounts of contaminants, derived from litter, garbage, car-washings, horticultural treatments, vehicle drippings, industry, construction, animal droppings and chemicals used for snow and ice clearance. in new york city some half million dogs leave up to 20,000 tonnes of pollutant faeces and up to 3.8 million litres of urine in the city streets each year, all of which is flushed by gutters to storm-water sewers... sewage is still a major pollutant. The new york metropolitan area alone produces 6.8 billion litres of sewage per day of which about 16 per cent is raw. much of this enters the hudson and east rivers around new york. in addition the city produces may tons of sewage sludge, fly ash and dredge waste per day, and 8.6 million tonnes of waste are dumped each year into the new york bight, off the mouth of the hudson river. In an area of about 100km2 there is a black toxic sludge which smothers all forms of marine life."
andrew goudie, *the human impact on the natural environment*

CRY VI

funeral of thomas à beckett (1118-70)
who was murdered in canterbury cathedral

"the body lay in the cathedral all night, and was prepared for burial on the following day. the archbishop was dressed, in an extraordinary collection of clothes. he had on a large brown mantle; under it, a white surplice; below that, a lamb's wool coat; then another woolen coat; and a third woolen coat below this; under this there was the black cowled robe of the benedictine order; under this a shirt; and next to the body a curious hair-cloth, covered with linen. as the body cooled, the vermin that were living in this multiple covering started to crawl out and 'boiling over like water in a shimmering cauldron', and the on lookers burst into alternative weeping and laughter…"
todd richardson, *plague, weather, and wool*
hans zinsser, *rats, lice and history*

newsflash:

on fox five news at ten, khalil, vivian and i were asked
vivian commented that we the neighbors had for years called for help she
called this in, dog ravished, parts of carcass strewn in backyard
he lived there with his dogs
the nypd pick axed the front door
he had suffered a stroke had been bitten by rats had been admitted to the hospital
13 pit bulls inbred alive covered with filth and mange
there were 24 dogs last summer
he had barricaded himself to avoid entrance
kim (his neighbor on the left) took photographs of the dogs cannibalizing the weaker dogs
dogs rats and alex lived in the three floor house no running water

insideoutside
internalexternal
heartsociety
innerearthouterspace
lipsasshole

department of health said
they lent me a hazmat suit so i could be a community witness
foot deep rotting matter fecal fetid no chair no table no toilet
he slept in the basement but i couldn't reach it the ground was unstable and the mounds of decay prohibitive
the house is condemned and he is homeless—staying with friends
gwen, neighbor adjacent, retired nypd detective said this syndrome is common
she'd witnessed
countless cases of animal abuse and cases where there was no separation between excrement and flesh
where pets would be neglected, without a food source, resort to eating their keepers
alex was a
dutiful worker at junior's didn't miss work wore waiter outfit black pants white shirt
went to the laundry once a week the department of sanitation sent teams of workers to excavate
they've been
working daily for over two weeks filling up dumpsters alex speaks 6 languages
received his degree from harvard used to love to see the new york city ballet with max another of our neighbors

'IN SO SAGACIOUS AN ANIMAL, WHATEVER ARISES
FROM THE EXERTION OF HIS INTELLECTUAL FACULTIES
MAY JUSTLY BE ESTEEMED NATURAL."
DAVID HUME, *ENQUIRY CONCERNING THE PRINCIPLES OF MORALS*

a particularly *expressive* gesture

saint augustine wrote, "christ himself shows that to refrain from the killing of animals and the destroying of plants is the height of superstition, for, judging that there are no common rights between us and the beasts and the trees, he sent the devils into a herd of swine and with a curse withered the tree on which he found no fruit."
john Passmore, *the catholic and manichean ways of life*

bonum est multiplex

constant disparagement of pigs what pigs are used as stand in symbols to represent

HOG WILD, ETC.

people to pig to people to pig triangle

labor recruitment
coercion
sexual management
biopolitics———**FOUCAULT: "HOW POWER RELATIONS ARE PLAYED OUT IN HOW BODIES ARE AGGREGATED, AND INDIVIDUATED, HEALED, BURIED, AND MADE INDISTINGUISHABLE AND MARKED."**

WOMEN WERE SEEN AS VEHICLES FOR TRANSMISSION, NOT ONLY OF LIFE BUT ALSO OF SPECIFIC CULTURAL ASSETS SUCH AS PROPERTY RIGHTS AND SOCIAL PRIVILEGE.
DIANA TAYLOR, *THE ARCHIVE AND THE REPERTOIRE, PERFORMING CULTURAL MEMORY IN THE AMERICAS*
racial taxonomies/animal taxonomies animal modernism

> **"note how even the syntax absents key actors. foucault makes no room for the fact that these bourgeois bodies were produced in practices never contingent on the will to self-affirmation alone. this 'body to be cared for, protected, cultivated, and preserved from the many dangers and contacts' required other bodies that would perform those nurturing services and provide the leisure for such self-absorbed administerings and self-bolstering acts. it was a gendered body and a dependent one, on that intimate set of sexual and service relations between french men and vietnamese women, dutch women and indo men and shaped by the politics of race. native women who served as concubines, servants, nursemaids, and wives in european households at once threatened the 'differential value' of adults' and children's bodies that they were there to protect and affirm."**
> **ann stoler, *carnal knowledge and imperial power***

u.s. social science where it implies eugenics: science calls this "trash"
congealed around the salt block show them dignity

live enactment

agribusiness: "boring into the domestic, familial and sexuality of cows"

> "my proper name is molly. i grew up in the country— had five brothers, two sisters. it was a happy childhood no want. i was loved by my parents. our youth was particularly idyllic as the definition goes we had a big meadow, much time for idyll play, few stressful elements."

eventually the farmer who owned us sold us off—my brothers were sold off for slaughter and myself
and two sisters, penned, milked until our nipples oozed, infectious, raw. we were pumped with antibiotics, hormones, trapped in the tiny cell ankles deep in excrement. the meadow became a housing subdivision for elderly urbanites. we were forced in the barn most days. it was a dismal existence, full of pain and suffering without reprieve. this is how we spent our days. my sister's hind quarters had mange. our eyes showed our hardship. we have a substance called milk, called meat. brides coat their lips with our hooves."

MONOLOGIC

METABOLISM
METABOLISM
METABOLISM.
METABOLISM:
METABOLISM:
METABOLISM:
METABOLISM:.
METABOLISM...

GENERALIZED OXEN

IN CARPETED ROOM WATCH *ANIMAL PLANET*

my parents watch the crocodiles on tv the man is flipped over by the gater, slow mo splash. incisors. the man is upright! he collects a fat sample and tags the gater. *first he tranquilzes the gater*. the gater is 18 feet long! his massive tail. his reptilian aura. the attention the camera gives to his gurgitation of a python.

pit

stop

the gas station where i stop to pee sells gummi sharks, gummi frogs and gummi bears the shelf where they are sold is closest to the restroom they have other animal shaped edibles too i haven't studied their inventory

drives ram into the ground

drops like flies

hyena

bower birds collect blue

fat cow / lard /
whore /
/ pig /
/ piece
/of meat /
chick /

"THE TRUTH IS—IN SEXIST AMERICA, WHERE WOMEN ARE OBJECTIFIED EXTENSIONS OF MALE EGO, BLACK WOMEN HAVE BEEN LABELED HAMBURGER AND WHITE WOMEN PRIME RIB."
BELL HOOKS, *AIN'T I A WOMAN: BLACK WOMEN AND FEMINISM*

"i feel guilty myself for an attack i made on olson while i was in buffalo. and i can see how in some way the feminist issue may do away with interest in olson by the young. because olson is far more extreme than melville on that subject. if there is WOMAN in olson's writing (there aren't women there), she is either "cunt," "great mother," "cow," or "whore." but the feminine is very much in his poems in another way, a way similar to melville. it's voice…it has to do with the presence of absence with articulation of sound forms. the fractured syntax, the gaps, the silences are equal to the sounds in maximus…"

susan howe, *the birth-mark unsettling the wilderness in american literary history*

joy chatel tells us the history of her house at 227 duffield street, downtown brooklyn, a slave safe house on the underground railroad. african americans and white women were given temporary sanctuary as they escaped bondage as slaves, indentured servants, sexual servants. the city wants to use eminent domain to demolish the house and build an underground parking lot for a new hotel, to be built by an out of state developer as part of the gentrification of brooklyn.

Whose whose is it this this
is it this of this that
is
land
porous
regulatory interchange
beware
interchange
where
where whose
wary
was built by
accredited

real an d
simulated l ife
manipulate d bowed
tang led;
centered and dispersed

MAD DOG———MADMAN?

T—HE

salt lick

whale bone

quick, gone

quick walk lane

hands betray

them

sing knelling

we *shhhhhhh*

caught them

never least

scant welt

abundance extremity

______________, _____________ being

foremost amongst them

provocative

alluring

never a substitution

surge internal, surge—syncretism, systems meld

"their soft meats cross the border"

barbara guest

(verb) of the (noun) at the heart of (same noun), the (new noun) maintains its strangle hold on the state apparatus thorough its increasing efforts to (new verb) and (new verb) (the new noun) in such a way that catch word is decentered with respect to the real places and deciding factors that (   ) so beyond states and point to the international capital economy
ecosystem where it *pays* to be aggressive

historical causality/subjugated group

liquidation/liquefaction

how will you be remembered by big other

you make the wall seem so close and timely— this animal involves flight

~~could my view~~ on this matter somehow
be so individuated
(salient) as to be only as good (salient)
as my own thought

is it in and of itself
important to be
a product of one's generation

so it was said
so it was spoken

CRY VII

(widespread endocrine destabilization)

physiological

sequestration/bodies

yet the recipe calls for three elbows
slather on the breast
if you gently pull skin away
marinate
goes easily
between the skin and flesh
preheat the ovens to 450°
(she) is the right weight and not too muscular
not too chewy she's resided in the smallest chamber
a four by two foot cell
pay no attention to the rotten foot
will be discarded at the slaughter house
cells will release toxicity, ummmmmm
she'd been feed a steady diet of the bones
of her ancestors mixed with corn, of course
that and a healthy, substantial round of fortifying agents
antibiotics, pain killers, anti-depressants, fat retainers
she represents the pride of the herd
name: sally

how this treats the body
legalese impacts bodies
raid deep
fallout vein

drones heat denial
shrapnel dislodges skull
through smog of commuters of jogs of
in the morning
spigot shutdown black out white out
town where i grew up: superfund sites cluster
welcome to a foot of a mountain
leukemia syndrome

the sign that said mercury sludge rotted away

lick rocks at your own risk

NORTH ADAMS MAD981065741	BERKSHIRE TANNING CO (FORMER)	ASHTON AVENUE
NORTH ADAMS MAD980906861	INFLATED PRODUCTS CO	MILL AND UNION STS
NORTH ADAMS MAD000846212	NORTH ADAMS LANDFILL	151 E STREET
NORTH ADAMS MAD980504039	NORTH ADAMS STP (CLOSED)	MASSACHUSETTS AVE
NORTH ADAMS MAD985279397	SHAPIRO	521 ASHLAND STREET
NORTH ADAMS MAD002067304	SPRAGUE ELECTRIC	87 MARSHALL STREET
NORTH ADAMS MAD000791038	SPRAGUE ELECTRIC CO	65 BROWN ST

(super fund sites within three miles our home—this author)

keep in mind, poor communities and communities of color suffer disproportionately from asthma, lead poisoning, developmental disorder and general environmental degradation————————————————————oh
right——————————that
——————————cancer————————————————————
cluster

poor and the load
poor poor load
loaded with the junk
the stuff
the lingering ejecta
the gunk that does not rid itself
that commands
the cells
the young men
head off to fight

during the vietnam war
2.4 million tons
of bombs were dropped
on ho chi minh trail
almost twice the amount us air forces
dropped on all of germany
during world war 2

factual victual virtual silence
farcical facial recognizance violence
intensest nature

supernormal tendency
today one's actions
conscientiously

owning up to intensification
owning up to implicit obligations
embedded within
the habitus of social
ecological space

a living future

our poor derelict town frowns
frowns upon clouds of waste and want
fraught upon what and down there
is how we milk the land

i grew up at 212 notch road
the above super sites don't include
removal of the *all the houses* situated on avon street
junction where notch road joins route 2
mysteriously
more than a half dozen
houses were bulldozed————
the ground, laden with pcbs
dumped sub rosa and ala and via deceased company: sprague electric

IF YOU SWIM IN THIS WATERING HOLE
YOUR BABIES WILL BE MUTANTS

local color: iron laden, copper sheen, magnesium cool, dull lead shade

"settled" in late 1700's
discounts humanity
(mohicans, pocumtuck, nonotuck and mohawks displaced, slaughtered,
decimated by small pox, measles, diphtheria, scarlet fever)

acute, through needles of pine
non fiction
existence/dissemblance

pain and suffering aggregates
compiles into
incredibly deep substance

if I may say so myself   *about*
collective experience

place foot here
reverberation   i do and do
place foot here   woodland path
reverberation

rowdy local lusty youth with pick-up trucks we stationed under trees
thick night sweat cracked beer cans swagger bonfires close calls to death
wrap your spine around sycamore skinny dip the reservoir
moon howl bay bras in brambles
mica and flint the pseudo water tour doleful deer peer through thick
hemlock stands your collarbone is protruding
you look like hell in flannel
ecstasy is the night
sky is soft with flourish
healing vegetative silence

that vault to heaven you are building
is interesting

chipboard springboard picture perfect

human density, how many?

CRY VIII

thin layers of rock relocated, edaphic (soil) conditions, shallow profile of soil, geomorphology of the area, export decomposable plant debris, buffer, erosion, logging operations, increased need for meat in the so-called first world, their bodies are enlarging, remove the forest for grazing, the diet calls for it, felling, pollen analysis shows that temperate forests were removed in the mesolithic and neolithic times and thereafter accelerated, continues to accelerate, agriculture, fuel, charcoal, smoking, wood for construction, smelting of metals, mining of ores, smelting of metals, short bodies, often tergal keels quadrangular flat-backs, tapers towards the ends, head usually subtriangular, cylindrical often with ridges and crests, narrow bodies, "beak" on head, coil around their eggs or young, mainly use silk only during mating and capturing prey, on males, the first pair of legs on the 7th ring are gonopods, which are copulating organs, feed on organic, decaying matter, mate throughout the year, some may crawl into swimming pools and drown. the young resemble the adults, except there are smaller and lighter in color. the female carries the eggs, numbering from 7 to 200 in a brood pouch on the underside of her body. sprays or dusts of bendiocarb (ficam), chlorpyrifos (duration, dursban, empire, engage), diazinon, propoxur (baygon), carbaryl (sevin), pyrethrins (exciter, kicker, microcare, pyrethrum, safer) or resmethrin (vectrin) are effective. other labelled pesticides include acephate (orthene), amorphous silica gel (drione, tri-die), boric acid (perma-dust) and esfenvalerate (conquer). treatment of peat moss, leaves and bark used as plant mulches is important. subsequent sprinkling with water will carry the pesticide down into the soil where these crustaceans hide. materials such as fluvalinate (mavrik, yardex) are used outdoors. mouthparts are modified for piercing and sucking, adults can survive starvation for a year or more, in certain conditions, eggs hatch in 10 days. the nymph stage lasts 6 weeks, and undergoes 5 molts. house centipedes feed on small insects, insect larvae, and on spiders. they are beneficial though most homeowners take a different point of view. natural predators include frogs, newts, toads and small mammals which live and hunt at night on the moist areas where pill bugs live. make valuable contribution to the

cockroaches

and

cockroaches cockroaches

mantids

and and

cockroaches

mantids cockroaches mantids

and

and

cockroaches cockroaches mantids

mantids

and and

cockroaches

mantids mantids

and

mantids

decomposition process. pill bugs are unusual dry-land crustaceans. beetles recycle rainforest nutrients, seething with life, saproxylic, hole nesting birds, cryptic, use green colors to imitate leaves, bugs: hemiptera, elongated snout (rostrum) drill into leaves create egg chambers paper wasp, leaf beetle, stag beetle, dragon fly, grasshopper, cicada, nature bee, rhinoceros beetle, huntsman spider, termite, whirligig beetle, green tree ant, forest cricket, katydids, stick insect, golden orb spider, fireflies, ladybirds, passalid beetles, ground beetles, aquatic beetles, longicorn beetles, rove beetles, weevils, ambrosia beetles, jewel beetles, metallic wood borers, hummingbird flower mite—they travel inside the hummingbird's nostril from flower to flower, army ants, grain beetle, pirate bug, christmas beetle, june bug, the ithystenus hoolandiae lives on the outside of logs and has an interesting sex life, the males which have unusually long legs, come in two sizes—large and small. the large male stands over his chosen mate, but the small male sometimes sneaks between his legs and mates with the female instead. like parrot fish, fossil beetle, blister beetle, southern pine beetle, fiddler beetle, crustacean: main body regions, two cephalothorax andabdomen, five or more pairs of legs, myriapoda: two main body regions: head and trunk, many legs, one or two pairs of legs per trunk segment, arachnida: two main regions: two cephalothoraz and abdomen, four leg pairs, insecta: three main body regions: head, thorax and abdomen, three pairs of legs, crustacean: order: isopoda oniscoidea, wood lice, water fleas (daphnia), fairy, brine, tadpole and clam shrimps, copepoda: water fleas (cyclops), fish lice, gill maggots, and an anchor worms, ostracoda: seed shrimps, cirrepedin: barnacles, stomatopoda: mantis shrimps, mysidacea: opossum shrimps, decapoda: shrimps, prawns, lobsters, cray fish and crabs, amphipoda: freshwater shrimps, gammarus, and sand hoppers, tsopoda: sea slaters, water slater, they nibble on dead matter that collects on rocky shores. scavengers, affected by reclamation and pollution. decomposition of faecal pellets contain fungal spores in deep moist leaf litter by woodlice is important in simulating decomposition in woodlands in the u.s., woodlice are used by museum workers to clear the flesh from delicate vertebrate skeletons. individual hemilepistus are able to walk several kilometers in a few days in a rigorous desert environment. graze on the microscopic plants floating in the sea. rice paddies, borrowing crabs and mud-eating shrimps, below waterline, planktonic larval stage, water lice and hog lice, myriapoda: centipede like creatures, pauropoda, symphyla, diplopoda: millipedes, chilopeda: centipedes, goliath beetle, at least 30,000 different types of scarab bettles, elytra: hard exoskeletal covering, faunal survey, cigarette beetle: feeds on a diversity of edible and non-edible products: spices, rice, dried pet food, seeds, pharmaceuticals, books, etc., tobacco products, larder beetle: her legs are covered with fine yellow hairs. food: ham, bacon, meats, cheeses, dried pet food, dried museum specimens of all kinds, dried fish, dried hides. class insecta: 29 orders: biting lice, sucking lice, true bugs, thrips, alder flies, snake flies or lacewings, beetles, stylopids, scorpion flies, fleas, true flies, butterflies and moths, caddis flies, bees, wasps and ants, bristle tails, two-pronged bristletails, springtails, mayflies, dragon flies, stone flies, crickets, grasshoppers and locusts, protura, grylloblattodea, stick and leaf insects, earwigs, web spinners, cockroaches and mantids, termites, zoraptera, psocoptera, book lice. arachnida: 8 orders: xiphosuran: king crabs or horseshoe crabs, pseudoscorpions: pseudoscorpions or false scorpions, scorpionidea: scorpions, pedipalpi: whip scorpions, solifuga: wind scorpions or barrel spiders, opilions: harvestmen or harvest spiders, acari: mites and ticks, araneae: true spiders. recovery of sinuosity as a result of bank erosion in channels with high slope gradients, peak flow of river

CRY IX:

figure 8.6

stressed out

"projected areas of flooding as a result of sea-level change in bangladesh, for two scenarios (low=1 m and high= 3 m). each dot represents 2000 persons at the time of the 1971 census."…florida, louisiana, new york, delaware, mississippi, alabama…"

vegetable belts

salivary glands, as with other mucosal glands, are largely under autonomic nervous system control. the preganglionic autonomic centers in the brain stem that regulate salivary gland activity receive direct inhibitory and excitatory inputs from neural structures in the forebrain that are part of recognized "stress circuits" and centers for homeostatic regulation. the salivary glands form a highly sophisticated endpoint in the CNS control of local immune defenses, capable of responding instantly and with a high level of specificity to potential source of harm (e.g., stress, inflammation). this remarkable ability, together with their strategic location at the portal of entry to the respiratory and gastrointestinal tract, make these glands ideally suited to provide the host with a first line of

defense. (24) odor from industrial hog farming operations and mucosal immune function in neighbors

rachel c. avery, steve wing, stephen w. marshall, susan s. schiffman,
archives of environmental health, feb, 2004

torsos meet in the emergency of fictive nuance
expedite animal before the encounter
the other as totally denaturing each comeback
molecular shift in emotional perspective
a modern militarized state, for animals, all
animals in the foreground and background
outside was always included as here
here was always value as in evaluated
always has to do with human animal apperception
when will be relearn our former languages?
a multispecies spectacle like growing up together
call me out as animal to declare grace
we'll be willing to meet you half way
ontologically departing from a delusional
categorical position fraught with genocidal history

surely makes you lose your mind...

cesspools of shame:

how factory farm lagoons and sprayfields threaten environmental and public health

this july 2001 report from NRDC and the clean water network documents how animal waste from factory farms threatens human health and our nation's rivers. most factory farms store animal waste in open lagoons as large as several football fields. lagoons routinely burst, sending millions of gallons of manure into waterways and spreading microbes that can cause gastroenteritis, fevers, kidney failure, and death. this report lists the track records of the largest polluters and recommends existing technology that is safer and more sustainable."miscellaneous other human activities appear to affect seismic levels. in johannesburg, south africa, for example, gold-mining and associated blasting activity have produced tens of thousands of small tremors, and there is a notable reduction in the number that occur on sundays, a day of rest. in staffordshire, england, coal-mining has caused increased seismic activity. there are also cases where seismicity and faulting can be attributed to fluid extraction, for example, in the oilfields of texas and california and the gasfields of the po valley in italy."

flattened rat bridgestone tire

cloud cover feedback/ice and snow cover albedo feedback/ocean-land-cryosphere-biosphere

mary somerville mary midgley

tsunami *where animals went*

subsidence

thickness of seam

where it came from where it went what it is made of

CRY X

epergne *head covered*
with snakes
prairie fauna

twelve headed gorgon draconian measures cut down by shrapnel qurna
drones heat raid deep
yes, i can see your mule cousins within you
resemblance—me to him
him to me: pygmalion effect piggish pork bellied
pig iron armor pig on a poke

EAT CROW

nature spears nature

the flying giraffeoid pterodactyl encephlopod or sidewinder chomping major grass

animal in coma coma political uproar at phase state

out of the animal's nipple
physiological
accelerate
sequestration/bodies **a characteristic...**

leach green nexus
instrumental efficient causes

social sequelae

restitution for

____

volatile volatilization

____

CROCODILE TEARS

lower the costs

desideration [of capital]
werewolf/vampire
threshold in any direction

cash cows

jump off financial records into
ecological surround
ecological surround
surrounded by numbers and records

now and again

time and again

death squads
ministry of interior
bunkered down
their heads were drilled on
its own momentum
low boil

cobra committee

combing nearby woods

in the early eighteenth century, disease was pushing an already sparse population out of the sandhills area that now houses fort bragg when a set of three wars devastated native communities

time maneuver **backbend** **mind warping shift**

whips
i crack the moccasins from around my legs
and lean back dancing
laughing in the flames

in the fire hot ashes there
i found a baby bird
a wet envelope of skin
jodi braxton, *conversations*

prompted by colonial conflicts over land, grazing, and trading rights, the tuscarora war led to

hee-haw locked jaw
screwdriver
pile driver infinity and beyond
ostensible purpose of militias

germs, weapons conflicts of over trade goods

history is here and rears

take back the time
clock ratchet organ value speak

spatial seconds

we remember you history speaks

position and intervening in its course

revolution of haitian slaves, 1791

the death, exile and domination of all of the colony's native peoples east of the appalachians by 1715. this opened the fayetteville area to european settlements, which increased rapidly in mid-century. the wars, however, led some of the survivors to align with the catawon, to form the grouping known as lumbee, and to communicate

historians commonly describe the early u.s. army as a constabulatory defined by its appointed job of "indian hunting" rather than defense of national borders.

animal pelts, lumber,

sugar, cotton, people, later tobacco

boll weevil

hair, arms, our necks, our backs

ostensible purpose

quest

insurrections

disenfranchised

forefathered directly onto bodies

> posthumously, the dangerous ambiguity of her image intensified…but when mapped onto the black female body,
>
> deborah richards, *last one out*

take back time-the
take back time-the
take back time-the

time it could take
time it could take
time it could take

like really reality
like really reality
like really reality

like real farewell human fraught
like real farewell human fraught
like real farewell human fraught

fought feigned humanity harm harrowing hub
fought feigned humanity harm harrowing hub
fought feigned humanity harm harrowing hub

end? inlet? embayment? estuary? rainbow bridge?
end? inlet? embayment? estuary? rainbow bridge?
end? inlet? embayment? estuary? rainbow bridge?

fought feigned humanity harm harrowing hub
fought feigned humanity harm harrowing hub

like real farewell human fraught
like real farewell human fraught

like really reality
like really reality

time it could take
time it could take

take back time-the
take back time-the

intensification

yesterday's

cumulative ... climatologist's daydream

micro gestures ... ecological phase alteration

psychic horizontal perspective

pressurized atmospheric conditions

strewn

washed up

buried

abandoned

fleeing

take back

take back

time-the

gone—

right here

obscured
we are here
they are gone
where once was where once was
animal you've
been here before
full-fledged
animal
always

right here

gone—

obscured
we are here
they are gone
where once was
animal you've
been here before
full-fledged
animal
always
obscured
we are here
they are gone
where once was
animal you've
been here before
full-fledged
animal
always
obscured
we are here
they are gone
where once was
animal you've
been here before
full-fledged
animal
always
obscured
we are here
they are gone
where once was
animal you've
been here before
full-fledged
animal
always

TAKE BACK TIME,
TAKE BACK TIME

take back time-the
take back time-the
take back time-the

time it could take
time it could take
time it could take

like really
reality
like really
reality
like really
reality

like real farewell human fraught
like real farewell human fraught
farewell human fraught

fought feigned humanity harm harrowing hub
fought feigned humanity harm harrowing hub
fought feigned humanity harm harrowing hub

end? inlet? embayment? estuary? rainbow bridge?
end? inlet? embayment? estuary? rainbow bridge?
end? inlet? embayment? estuary? rainbow bridge?

take back time-the

like really reality

real

farewell human fraught

FAREWELL HUMAN FRAUGHT

fought feigned humanity harm harrowing hub

farewell human fraught

farewell human fraught

farewell human fraught

farewell human fraught

Brenda Iijima's involvements occur at the often unnamable conjunctions and mutations of poetry, ecological inquiry, research movement, visual art, animal studies and subsumed histories. She is the author of six full-length collections of poetry including *Early Linoleum* and *If Not Metamorphic* as well as numerous chapbooks and artist's books. She is the editor of the *eco language reader* and editor of Portable Press @ Yo-Yo Labs. She has taught at The Cooper Union and Naropa University.

NIGHTBOAT BOOKS

Nightboat Books, a nonprofit organization, seeks to develop audiences for writers whose work resists convention and transcends boundaries. We publish books rich with poignancy, intelligence, and risk. Please visit our website, www.nightboat.org, to learn about our titles and how you can support our future publications.

The following individuals have supported the publication of this book. We thank them for their generosity and commitment to the mission of Nightboat Books:

Elizabeth Motika
Benjamin Taylor

In addition, this book has been made possible, in part, by grants from The National Endowment for the Arts, and The New York State Council on the Arts Literature Program.

National
Endowment
for the Arts
arts.gov